SECRETS

True Stories
Of
Love, Lust and
MURDER

SECRETS

True Stories
Of
Love, Lust and
MURDER

KEN H. FORTENBERRY

SECRETS: True Stories of Love, Lust and Murder
By Ken H. Fortenberry

Printed in the United States of America

ISBN: 9798872005322

PREFACE

As an author always in search of good stories to tell, especially those based on facts and lost to history, I was immediately drawn to two unusual stories that were headline-screamers when they made news more than one hundred years ago.

Now, I am sharing them with you.

Both murders occurred within a few miles of each other in quiet farming communities in the Mountain Creek Township in Catawba County, North Carolina. The details of the crimes were as different as night and day, and the outcomes were entirely different as well. Still, they shared a common theme: love, lust, and jealousy.

The first story, *White Beauty, Black Beast,* is the sad and truly sensational story of Sarah Eller Wycoff and Robert McCorkle.

It isn't as simple as black and white.

After research that took me all over western North Carolina searching for records in the dusty nooks and crannies of courthouse basements, I still can't say with confidence that I know for certain happened on Thursday night, November 7, 1878, when Sarah's husband was shot to death in their front yard. During my research, I discovered that her murdered husband, John Wesley Wycoff, was a distant cousin of mine.

After talking with state and local officials and state archivists, and after studying hundreds of contradictory old newspaper clippings, I am still not convinced that all of the right people were brought to justice for the murder that shook the Tar Heel state and made headlines halfway across the country.

The story is confusing, yet quite simple in some ways. It happened during Reconstruction but is timely even today: A beautiful young married farm woman fell in love with a widower who lived nearby. Their affair ended in the murder of the woman's husband, a murder both lovers were accused of plotting and carrying out.

The twist to the story is that the beautiful married woman was white, and her lover was black.

How did a beautiful, young woman end up in the arms of a person someone described as a "an old, ungainly, coal-black, ugly, worthless negro" nearly three times her age?

Was it true love? Was it purely lust? Was it greed or something entirely different?

Did the former enslaved farmer Bob McCorkle take advantage of a lonely, neglected and sometimes abused housewife and conspire with her to kill her husband?

Was the stunning Sarah Wycoff really nothing more than a loose woman with many lovers who manipulated McCorkle to get what she really wanted – the death of a husband she never loved?

I have attempted to answer these questions and many more in *White Beauty, Black Beast*, and I'll leave it to you to reach your own conclusions about what actually happened. Sometimes, right and wrong, black and white, are in the eyes of the beholder.

Unlike *White Beauty, Black Beast*, the tale of Kohler Holdsclaw, is pretty straightforward, occasionally heartwarming, and sometimes chilling.

Hiding in Plain Sight captures the life of a young war veteran-turned fugitive who was convicted of killing a well-respected married man who made unwanted advances on the young woman he dearly loved and intended to marry. The condemned man disappeared twice but was always hiding in plain sight.

Both short stories are based on facts, but much of the dialogue in each has been created out of necessity or to make the stories clearer to read or easier to understand. In nearly every case, however, the dialogue is based upon printed reports or what few historical records still exist.

Creative nonfiction, they call it.

Hope you enjoy.

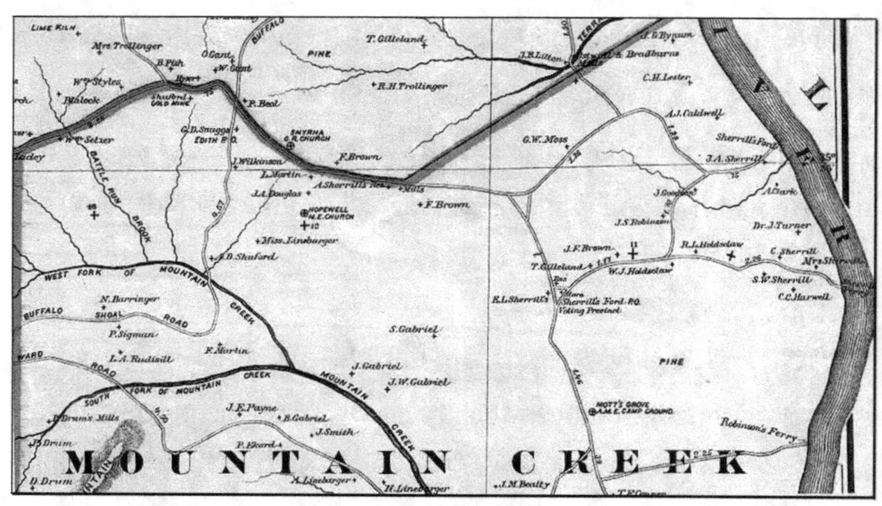

**1886 map of the Mountain Creek Township
. . . both murders occurred here.**

**The old Connor Store in Terrell, North Carolina
. . . the murder scene of John Gabriel**

White Beauty,
Black Beast

Chapter One

A Recipe for Murder

Taylorsville, North Carolina

Thursday, August 14, 1879

Bob McCorkle begged him not to leave. Down on a trembling right knee, hands folded tightly in the praying position, Bob pleaded.

"Please, Preacher. Just stay with me a little bit longer. Please, I'm begging you, sir. I don't want to be alone. Not tonight, especially not tonight. Please!"

It was almost midnight in the Alexander County Jail and the smelly kerosene lamp on the cellblock's hallway floor flickered ominously, a tell-tale sign of what was looming.

"I been hearing de hammers and de nails outside all day today, Preacher. Every time I hear a hammer pound into a nail over yonder, I get the shivers. I 'spect they 'bout got them gallows finished and the hangman is practicin' his knot-tyin' right now. The sheriff told me they're gonna make me sit on my own coffin and ride a buggy full of shotgun-totin' deputies to the hangin' place. Did you know that, Preacher? Make me sit on top of my own coffin?"

The preacher nodded.

"I heered tell that the white folks out there are calling me a jiggaboo and someone told a newspaper that I was the most God-awful looking creature he'd ever seen. How about that? Did you know that, Preacher? Them's probably some of the same folks who was on my jury."

The preacher ignored him. What could he say?

Bob's spiritual adviser prayed with him once more, then slowly stood up, wiped some straw from his pants and motioned to the jailer who had been keeping watch while seated in a nearby chair outside Bob's cell.

"I gotta go, Bob. I've already been here an awful long time and I gotta get home to the missus. I'll see you in the morning. God bless you, brother."

"You promise, Preacher? You'll come back in the mornin'?"

"I'll be here early, so help me God," he responded.

As soon as he uttered those words, the preacher regretted them. What was he thinking, he said to himself. "So, help me, God." How senseless.

The preacher turned and looked at the pitiful-faced Bob as the cold steel doors clanged, shutting the men off from each other, and for Bob, shutting him even further away from the world outside.

He reached his big, black calloused hands between the bars, furiously wiggled his begging fingers, and pleaded one more time.

"Please, Preacher. Please!" he begged as the jailer snuffed out the light, leaving Bob and the cell in pitch-black darkness and a sudden chill on an otherwise warm summer night.

"Please!"

It was no use. Bob was alone now, alone for what might be the last, desperate hours of his life.

He shuffled back and forth across the tiny cell, looking up at the ceiling, down at the floor, shaking his head left-to-right and singing softly to himself.

"Go down, Moses, way down in Egypt's land,
Tell old Pharaoh: Let my people go.
Let my people go."

Bob plopped down on the thin, straw-filled mattress on the floor and finally began to accept his fate. He rested his sweaty head in his thick, scarred and leather-skin hands and began to cry softly to himself. But stubborn as always, he quickly arose and paced the floor again, singing, praying, and wondering how he had come to this wretched place and why he had so easily given up everything and everybody he had loved to satisfy his own sinful lust and selfishness.

He didn't really blame anyone for his mistakes, but still he wondered how he had fallen, or had been lured, into the deep pit that had led him to this end.

"What the Hell was I thinking?" he screamed.

"What? Why? Why?"

Outside the wood-frame jail on dusty, red-dirt Main Avenue, a small crowd was already beginning to gather. They would be curious spectators at tomorrow's public spectacle, notices having been issued in newspapers far and wide, urging everyone to come to see for themselves how a man dies as he dangles at the end of a tight rope.

From all over the countryside, men, women, and children were traveling to the tiny farming village for the once-in-a-lifetime opportunity that would resemble more of a county fair or a Holy Ghost church spiritual revival than a final, solemn judicial proceeding.

The night was sweltering-hot one-hundred-forty miles to the east, far from the rolling green hills of Taylorsville. Sarah Eller Wycoff was keenly aware of both the date and what tomorrow would bring.

She looked at the calendar hanging on the cinder block wall beside her metal-frame bed and saw that tomorrow was circled. Twice.

Inside her cell in the women's prison unit in Raleigh, North Carolina, state inmate number 1304, held her Bible closely to her bosom and worried about the man she called "her Bob. She began to whimper as tears fell onto her face.

She, too, was alone tonight, but she would live to see tomorrow, and fifteen thousand more tomorrows – forty-one more years - before she would finally be set free.

The kind-hearted, quiet inmate thought about those exciting, breathtaking, and yes, dumb and reckless days, not so long ago, when she was foolish and in love.

In love with the wrong man.

She thought about the last time she and "her Bob" had been together, how they had crept quietly, separately, and secretly into the thick pine-and-oak woods near her Sherrills Ford home and rendezvoused one last time at an old tree stump. She had been giddy, careless and it had cost her dearly.

She remembered how they had feverishly kissed, how they had hugged, and how they had dreamingly talked about how wonderful their lives would be once the deed had been done and how they would live happily ever after.

Together, forever.

Forever never came. Now, separately, they were living in a hell they alone created.

She put away the pretty blue scarf she had been knitting, curled her body in bed, and cried herself to sleep. Sarah had accepted her fate ten months ago in a tense, spectator-filled Taylorsville courtroom and had never complained once.

"I'm keepin' our promise, Bob," she wept. "I'll always keep our promise."

Bradford Robert "Bob" McCorkle was no stranger to being deprived of his freedom. In fact, he had been born into the chains of slavery, one of dozens of enslaved African Americans on the plantation of the powerful, prestigious, and wealthy McCorkle family of Lincoln and Catawba counties.

Born in 1815, he and his parents assumed the same last names as their owners as was the custom in those days, and they knew little of the world beyond the McCorkle plantation. From dawn until dusk, they picked cotton until their hands bled, and worked the corn and wheat fields on the west side of the Catawba River where their owner, Francis Marion McCorkle Jr., oversaw his vast holdings. It was a huge farming empire that had been in his family for generations.

Plantation owner Francis McCorkle's father had been a North Carolina militia major in the Revolutionary War and had valiantly fought at the battles of Kings Mountain, Cowpens, Cowan's Ford, and Ramsour's Mill. He returned to the family plantation as a hero, and by all accounts was a privileged, well-respected citizen, a pleasant person and not prone to abusing his slaves. They were, after all, very valuable property on the thousands of acres he farmed.

Slave Bob grew into a big, burly man and he worked hard on the plantation both as a carpenter and as a fieldhand from childhood into adulthood. In 1852, he was permitted to marry twenty-seven-year-old Avaline (her last name is lost to history) even though he was ten years her senior. They had a son, Sim, not long afterwards, and that pleased both master and parents.

Another slave. Another hand to work the fields.

Bob and Avaline had five more children while enslaved on the McCorkle plantation: Brad, Neely, Jane, Mark, and Abe. Two more children, Samuel and Dice were born after slavery ended.

By some accounts, the plug-ugly and coal-black Bob, was hard-headed man, stubborn, proud and had a big mouth. One newspaper referred to him "an ungainly African of more than ordinary intelligence."

After the Civil War ended and the enslaved had been freed, Bob, now in his 50s with eight children, took on the mantle of "Doctor

Bob" and became prominent and active in Republican Party politics. He was a frequent stump speaker at Reconstruction-era political events in the black communities of eastern Catawba County, and drew the ire of many white Democrats, fearful of uppity blacks who were no longer under their control and had gained political power, were buying land, and threatening their racial purity and their way of life.

Many believed that the emancipated blacks, men in particular, were forcing them to lose grip on everything they held dear, from their property to their wives, some of whom they said were being targeted by the "black beasts" to feed their legendary sexual appetites.

Their hysteria and paranoia began to consume Catawba County from Scronce's village in the west to the numerous small farming villages along the Catawba River in the east.

Bob frequently tested the limits of his new-found freedom, and the more he tested, the further he backed himself into a corner. He knew that one day he might be urging a crowd of former slaves to vote and become active in local politics and the next day his castrated body might be swinging from a noose and whacked and sliced into pieces to punish him and to send a message to others.

He'd heard the stories. Every black person in Catawba had heard the stories about brutal beatings and lynchings by cowardly men who wore white hoods and snuck up to houses in the middle of the night to terrorize anyone – black, white, male, and sometimes even female - who dared to challenge their authority or their high moral standards. But the hard-headed ex-slave was willing to take the risks, even knowing that the Ku Kluxers had been active for several years and he might be next on their list.

He rejoiced in his freedom.

Loud, proud.

Maybe too loud. Too proud.

On more than one occasion, he is reported to have said these words that may have come back to haunt him years later: "White and black must eat, vote and sleep together."

For several years, Bob, Avaline, and the McCorkle children farmed in the Mountain Creek community not far from the former McCorkle plantation. He worked hard, saved his money, and ultimately rented a small piece of land just north of Sherrills Ford. It was near to the farm owned by John Wesley Wycoff, the man he would later be accused of murdering in cold blood.

Sarah Eller and Bob McCorkle's early lives were as different as black and white.

Sarah Eller was a beautiful baby who turned into a stunningly alluring woman. The third of five children born to farmer/miller Jeremiah and Annie Remer Eller, she came into the world in 1842 and was raised in a loving family of second-generation Americans. Her father's family had emigrated from Germany to Pennsylvania, and like many of that time, traveled south on the Great Wagon Road to North Carolina where they settled down and raised families in the backcountry.

Nothing is known of Sarah's early life, but on January 9, 1866, the twenty-four-year-old fetching strawberry blonde-haired, blue-eyed beauty married thirty-eight-year-old widower John Wesley Wycoff. Sarah moved into John's house in the Mountain Creek community and was a loving and devoted homemaker for the early years of their marriage and was a good mother to John's two sons, Charles and William, from his previous marriage to Polly, who had died several years earlier.

Three years after their marriage, on August 25, 1869, Sarah bore John a son they named Jacob. He would be their only child.

Sarah was head-strong and easy on the eyes. She turned men's heads everywhere she went in Terrell, Ball's Creek, Sherrills Ford and in the nearby railroad town of Catawba Station. John, whom some in the community called "old man Wycoff," had been wounded twice while serving with North Carolina's 49th Infantry in the Civil War and was prone to drink excessively after he came home from the war. He grew increasingly jealous, and when other men admiringly looked Sarah over and sometimes made lewd comments, he often went into a rage, taking it out on her.

"Dammit, woman!" he said one afternoon as some leering men sat on a bench outside Long's General Store and whistled, eyeing her from head to toe.

They heard John's harsh admonishment of his wife and looked in another direction, pretending not to hear.

"Quit sashaying around like that. You hear me, woman? I've had enough of that."

"I didn't do nothin'. Honest, John. I didn't. I was just walkin' like I always do."

"Then do it different."

"I can't help the way I walk."

"You damn sure can, and you damn sure will. I'm tired of you cavortin' around all the time."

"I don't even know what that word means, John."

They loaded their goods into the beaten-up buckboard wagon and didn't say a word for nearly an hour, slowly making their way on the two-rut dirt path that headed southeast through the tall pine trees and ancient oaks towards their little farm. Now and then, John glanced over at Sarah, knowing full well why the men at the general store admired her so. She *was* a beauty, what some men might call a "fiery beauty," and she couldn't be trusted. Not for a damned second.

She had innocent, flashing blue eyes and underneath her tattered farm clothes, her body was as stunning and as inviting as it had been on their wedding day. He admitted to himself that he might also have whistled at her as she walked by if he had been sitting with the men outside the store, and she hadn't been his wife.

And those innocent eyes. Those eyes. John knew they were hiding something.

After a few swigs of sow paw whiskey from a jug he kept in the barn, he would teach her another lesson tonight, and he told himself that maybe this time she would quit acting like a shameless tart every time she was out in public.

In late afternoon they passed by the old Wycoff homestead on Ball's Creek where John had grown up, and shortly before nightfall, they passed by Turner Abernethy's place, Ern Cornelius's farm, the Holdsclaw place, and the small farm where the recently widowed Bob McCorkle lived with his brood of children.

Sarah slowly turned her head in that direction, trying not to let her husband see.

"What are you looking at, woman?"

"Nothin.' "

"Bullshit."

"John, what in the world are you talkin' about?"

"I see the way he looks at you," John snarled.

"I can't help the way somebody looks at me."

"Maybe. Maybe not, but I don't like it. I don't like it one damned bit. Bob McCorkle is just like you. He's runnin' his mouth all over the county talkin' about blacks and whites eatin' together, livin' together, even gettin' married and such. We gotta put an end to that kind of talk around here. Dammit, woman, he's one of them troublemakers who got that nigger constitution passed over in Raleigh. Somebody needs to tear his hide up or string his black ass up an oak tree."

"Really, John? His black ass as you call it has worked for you lots of times on the farm. You even said that he was a good hand, and y'all even go huntin' together. He's even et vittles with us a bunch of times, 'specially since his wife up and died a while back. What you got against him all of a sudden?"

"You know damned well, woman. He's trouble. Big trouble and I ain't sayin' no more right now. You're gittin' me all riled up."

"Do tell, John," she urged. "Maybe the preacher from Rehobeth will talk about it on Sunday. He might even find sumpin' in the Good Book that talks about them trouble-making niggers you're always bitchin' about."

"Oh, shut up, Sarah. You know what the Hell I'm talking about. A woman ain't got no right to talk to her man like you do. I ought to slap your damned face for talkin' to me like that."

"You've done it before. Ain't no reason to think you ain't gonna do it again. Go ahead, John. Slap me. Slap me! It don't make no difference. You're gonna do what you're gonna do."

John reached over, drew back his fist and started to smack her, but Sarah quickly slid away and evaded his attack. She knew that things were quickly spinning out of control, and tried to change the subject, but egged him on just the same.

"Speakin' of church, why don't we go to church meetin' Sunday, John? That new preacher from over at Oxford's Ford is supposed to be there. I heered tell he was purty good. It might do us all good to go to church, especially the young 'uns," she pleaded.

"Shut up."

Sarah's irritation was beginning to boil over. She hesitated – always hesitated – to speak her mind because she knew what would happen if she pressed him too much, but she went ahead.

"What ails you anyway? You talk to ever body else, but you don't never talk to me no more."

"I said you talk too much, woman. You do all the talking, all the time. Ain't no time for me to get a word in."

"I knowed you got hurt in the war, got your leg shot up or sumpin' else even. That was afore I met you, but those nightmares – you have 'em all the time. There's sumpin' else, ain't there, John? There's gotta be sumpin' else. You've' done changed so much. Why won't you ever tell me about what happened in that war?"

"Stop it. It ain't got nothin' to do with that damned war, and that ain't none of your business anyway. I've done told you a hundred times, the war's over. We lost, and we're still payin' for it. Damned Yankees. The niggers are votin' and are in running everything from here to Raleigh these days."

"John . . ."

"Enough, woman. Enough!"

"How did his wife die anyways?"

"Whose wife?"

"Bob McCorkle. Who did you think I was askin' about?"

"I dunno. I don't care. Don't nobody care. Just a nigger woman who died. Might have been consumption. Happens all the time these days. Some was a sayin' that he might have killed her."

Sarah froze. Her hands began to tremble.

John grumbled something but said nothing more until they reached their farm. He unhitched the horse from the buggy and the

Wycoff children helped unload their few supplies that included flour, salt ("too gawl-darn expensive" he had said), coffee, beans, nails, and a few sewing notions Sarah insisted they buy.

"You're always sewin'. We can't afford that stuff," he had complained as she had put her goods on the general store counter.

"Kids gotta have sumpin' to wear."

After the buggy was unloaded, John trudged to the barn and grabbed the jug of whiskey that he had bought at Alley's Distillery over near Statesville. He lifted it into the air, rested it on his right arm, then chugged and chugged some more. He glared over at his log-frame house and decided that Sarah would pay a high price for her sassy and rebellious tongue tonight.

All of the ingredients were falling into place that would shred both the Wycoff and the McCorkle families into bits and scatter the remains into oblivion.

Lust.

Love.

Jealousy.

Simple as black and white.

The recipe for cold-blooded murder was ready to be prepared.

Bob heard the sound of horses' hooves and their high-pitched neighs minutes after he climbed into bed but before he drifted off. Startled and now wide awake, he ducked down and lit a candle beside his bed, then snuck on his hands and knees into the main room of his cabin. He heard the rustling of leaves outside and grew tense and boldly unfearful at the same time.

He had a feeling about what was to come.

His oldest boy, Sim, had also heard the commotion outside and rushed into the room.

"Get down!" his father loudly whispered, "and tell them young 'uns to lay low and be quiet."

"What's going on, Papa?"
"Hush, I tell you. Get down and be quiet!"

The sound of a horse approached the porch and the light of a hand-held gas lantern sneaked into the open crevices on the bottom and sides of the doorframe.

"Nigger!" a booming male voice cried out. "Nigger, we know you're in there!"

What sounded like a huge chunk of wood smashed loudly into the worn-out door that rattled with the thump.

Bob ducked his head down even further but didn't make a sound or utter a word.

"Nigger, we ain't tellin' you no more. Stay away from that Wycoff woman or any other white woman around here or you're dead! Dead, I tell you. You'll be dead and hanging from one of these trees out here."

"What's he talkin' about, Papa?' Sim asked.

"Hush, boy. Hush," Bob admonished.

They both heard the riders slap their reins, and in an instant the sound of horses disappeared into the night.

Now quick desire hath caught the yielding prey,
And glutton-like she feeds, yet never filleth;

Her lips are conquerors, his lips obey,
Paying what ransom the insulter willeth;

Whose vulture thought doth pitch the price so high,
That she will draw his lips' rich treasure dry.

- *Venus and Adonis by William Shakespeare*

Chapter Two

Forbidden Fruit

Sarah didn't consider herself some kind of Jezebel; she was just a lonely, and in some ways a homely, yet dashing woman with an older husband who often neglected and sometimes abused her.

She needed and deserved to be loved.

That's what she told herself nearly every day.

She had never really loved John anyway. Theirs was more a marriage of convenience than love. He needed someone to care for his two growing boys and she wanted to leave her parents' home and not become a childless old maid like that Brotherton woman who lived nearby.

Early in their marriage, they got along well enough, but there was never any tenderness, never any love. The hard-working John was never the loving kind.

Unfulfilled, drained, and just plain miserable for the past few years, Sarah's mundane life was eating away at her mind, her body, her soul. She had to do something. Her spirit was dying, and she yearned to keep it alive.

Like her husband, she had little of what they called "book-learning" but that didn't mean she was dumb. Far from it. Life on the farm was hard and a formal education was not only unnecessary but was also considered by most in the community to be a waste of perfectly good time.

She could read well enough to read the Bible when she could find the time, which was not very often. She may not have understood everything she read in The Good Book, but she understood enough to know there were sinners 'a plenty inside its pages, and that their sins, although shameful, were forgiven if a person accepted Jesus, and she had done that at a little Baptist church near Monbo when she was barely nine years old. She wasn't quite sure how long that baptism-day forgiveness was supposed to last, but she hoped it lasted a long, long time.

Sarah was proud of her handwriting, but she had no one to send a letter, so she mostly just made notes in her Bible.

On the outside, she was just like hundreds of other farm women who lived in the Mountain Creek Township: a simple, hard-working, quiet, dutiful wife and mother who knew her place.

On the inside, though, Sarah was a determined woman with a head full of common sense and a growing and restless impatience for something more in her life. She knew little of the world outside her tiny farming community, but what she did know teased her, and teased her in many ways, some of them so embarrassingly shameful that she put them out of her mind as soon as they entered.

Up before dawn on this frosty morning, she brushed her hair, tidied herself up a bit then rekindled a fire in the wood-burning stove before heading outside to toss a bucket of swill to the stock hogs in a pen near the old barn where they kept four cows and one old mare.

"Lord, I pray those hogs don't die afore butcherin' time," she said aloud. "Cholera's been getting' a lot of 'em around here. We can't afford to lose any, Lord. None."

On her way back to the cabin she gathered some freshly laid eggs and placed them carefully in her bundled-up apron. John insisted on two eggs fried in pork fat every morning before he went to work, and this morning she actually looked forward to preparing his breakfast and scooting him out the door. Today, John planned to leave the farm for several days to do some carpentry work for a

Jewish merchant over in Hickory Tavern. She would be on her own, performing not only her farm chores, but John's as well.

The younger boys, William, and Jacob did their fair share around the farm, but it often required a stern warning, followed by a switch to their squirming legs. Jacob, especially Jacob, was the most difficult to control. He had a mean streak that even a whoopin' from a two-foot hickory switch couldn't quell. The oldest boy, Charlie, was seldom a problem and kept mostly to himself when he wasn't working on the farm or staying with his grandparents who lived near Catawba Station where his grandfather, Joseph T. Sanders, was the town's blacksmith.

"William and Jake oughtta go to that log schoolhouse on the hill a lot more than they do, John. It ain't that far away. They ain't learnin' nothin' around here except how to raise corn, wheat, some oats and how to slop them damned hogs," she had pleaded once.

"Dammit! Them damned hogs as you call them, put food on the table. And learnin' what, woman? All they need to learn is right on this farm. All a man needs is right here in front of his own eyes. Open yours up. They don't need to know nothin' else."

"My eyes or the boys?"

"Shut up, Sarah."

"You know what I mean, John. There's a big, wide world out there," she said, her eyes brightening up with the very thought. "The world don't end at the Catawba River or over in Hickory Tavern. Don't you ever want to stand on the top of a mountain or walk on a sandy beach somewhere and see the waves?"

"You're talking foolish, woman, and I've seen that big world you keep talkin' about," he hurled back. "There's nothin' but trouble out there. I've walked and soldiered from here to Virginny, and there's nothing' but trouble out there. Trouble and big-talkin' Yankees who'd just as soon rob you as look at you."

"Come on, John. Ever body's not like that, and the war's done been over a long time. The Yankees as you call 'em are Americans just like us."

"Bullshit, woman. You're beginnin' to sound just like Charlie, always talkin' about somethin' outside of the farm, like them folks loadin' timber and cattle into those loud freight trains up there in Catawba. And them people getting' on them passenger cars? Well, they're likely headin' to God-knows-where for God-knows-what and I don't care to have none of that."

"Ain't nothin' wrong with dreamin'," she said.

Then, he uncharacteristically compromised.

"Tell you what, woman. If you'll stop naggin' me about it all the damned time, I might let the boys go to that schoolhouse a little more this winter, but only when there ain't no work to do on the farm. I ain't promisin', though."

"Thank you, John. That'd be a big heap of help to those boys as they get older. They might want to leave the farm one day and they'll need some learnin.' "

Stunned by her slight victory and the thought of having some time alone, Sarah smiled to herself and said not another word. Let John think he was doing something good for a change.

There were plenty of farm chores for her to do all day long, every single, blessed day, but first she had to take care of her other duties this morning: breakfast for John and the boys.

Feeding and watering the chickens, sweeping the floors, milking the cows, washing and mending clothes, working in the garden, gathering firewood, fixing supper. Those things would have to wait until after John had left for Hickory Tavern and the boys went off to that schoolhouse on the hill.

Today, she would insist they go to that schoolhouse.

But for now, it was work, work, work.

Most nights Sarah went to bed with a mind-bending headache, a powerful backache, and on those nights that John treated her like a common farm hand, she cried herself to sleep with a deep heartache.

Lately, those heartaches had been coming more frequently, and before she had drifted off to sleep last night, she lay awake in bed, tossing, turning, and wondering if she would ever have the kind of life she had dreamt about as a little girl growing up on her daddy's farm.

But today, today would be her day. She rushed to get the morning chores done, singing merrily along the way:

"Camptown ladies sing dis song, Doo-dah! doo-dah!
Camptown race-track five miles long, Oh, doo-dah day!
I come down dah with my hat caved in, Doo-dah! doo-dah!
I go back home with a pocketful of tin, Oh, doo-dah day!

Goin' to run all night,
Goin' to run all day!
I'll bet my money on de bob-tail nag,
Somebody bet on the bay"

She knew he was coming. He always did.

Sarah piddled around the kitchen for a good hour after John had left and the boys had walked off to school, then slightly cracked a window and draped an old washrag over the top pane. She smiled, then loosely closed the window, leaving it open enough for the washrag to blow ever so slightly when a breeze drifted by. It was chilly outside, but she felt warm all over.

Hiding among some sourwoods and black gums about forty yards away, Bob squinted and stared at the Wycoff house. Thin gray smoke seeped out of the stone chimney, and he crouched lower, pulling his worn-out coat tightly around his chest and his trusty shotgun even closer.

Then he thought he saw something but had to sneak a bit closer to the house to be sure. Quietly, like a deer in a forest, he drew closer and closer.

Yes, it was there all right.

The sign. The old dishrag. It was safe.

It was the same as always. Talking quietly. Hugging. Kissing. Then sex.

But there was something else: tenderness. Bob coddled, pampered, and showered Sarah with affection. He always treated her with respect and sometimes playfully dipped his head and called her "Miss Sarah."

She could never say the same about how John treated her, and although it was illegal, immoral, and absolutely sinful in the eyes of God, Sarah felt alive when she was in Bob's arms, and she could dream.

MURDERED.—A horrible murder was committed in Catawba county, near Sherrill's Ford, the early part of this week. Mr Wesley Wycoff was called into his yard at night by the barking of dogs, and was shot and killed by some one in the yard. A negro named Bob McCorkle has been arrested and committed to Jail under strong suspicion, and Wycoff's wife also committed as an accessory. The gun wadding found near the dead body was the same piece of paper given the negro at a store that day, and the wadding found in the newly loaded gun of the negro corresponded with that fired from the gun that killed Wycoff.

"The eye of the adulterer waits for the twilight, saying, 'No eye will see me.' And he disguises his face."   *- Job 23:15*

Chapter Three

Death in the Castle

Thursday, November 7, 1878

Comfortably seated in his fireside chair, John Wesley Wycoff whittled on a piece of freshly cut hickory wood and neither talked nor looked at anyone in the room. His belly was full of supper, and a couple of swigs of corn liquor that he had swallowed like a glutton a few minutes earlier brought a slight grin to his dirty face.

It was close to 8 p.m. and the darkness of early fall had come swiftly after an exhausting day working on the farm.

He was a man in his castle. King of the roost.

Sarah and the boys chattered nearby but he paid them no mind. Never really did.

Suddenly, he heard the furious loud yelping of a dog outside. Something or someone was out there!

"What in tarnation is that this time of night?" he asked and quickly got out of his chair, heading directly for the door. He opened it, peered outside, and seeing nothing, shook his head and walked off the small porch and out into the yard.

He didn't see the fire or the smoke that came out of the barrel, but he heard the loud roar of a shotgun as bits of wadding and lightning-hot pellets ripped into his body.

"Lord, have mercy on my soul!" he screamed, then fell flat on his face.

Sarah and the boys froze, and even after the shock of what might have just happened settled in, they did not dare go outside. They sat in silence, and after several minutes, Jake finally spoke up.

"Mama, we need to go out there. Papa needs our help!" he pleaded.

"No, child. Ain't nobody going out there until we know it's safe."

"But, Mama. . ."

"Jake, your pap's killed."

Stunned and afraid for their lives and what might happen to them if they stepped outside where an assailant had just attacked, the children sat nervously, and numb. Sarah assumed John's place in his chair and occasionally dozed before standing up and yawning innocently as dawn broke.

"I'm goin' out now," she said. "Gonna get some help."

She made her way to a cabin rented by a black family nearby and told her neighbors that her husband had been shot. They rushed back to Wycoff place, but by the time they arrived, Sarah's husband was beyond help.

John Wesley Wycoff was lying in a pool of coagulating blood, arms sprawled at his side.

Stone-cold dead.

The news of Wycoff's murder spread like wildfire throughout the community within hours and nearly everyone had the same suspects in mind. On Monday, four days after his Wycoff's death, the Catawba County coroner convened an inquest, and after hearing testimony and viewing evidence including Wycoff's body, he ordered the arrest of Bob McCorkle for murder and Sarah Wycoff as accessory to murder. Deputies arrested them without incident, and they were placed in Catawba County's jail in Newton by Wednesday night. On Thursday, a motion was filed in Catawba County Superior Court to hold a preliminary hearing for the suspects.

"Enough evidence was elicited at the coroner's inquest, held over the body of Wesley Wycoff, to cause the arrest of Bob McCorkle, colored, commonly known as 'Dr. Bob,' who carries his gun wherever he goes since emancipation," a newspaper reported. "Mrs. Wycoff, wife of the deceased, was also put in the lock-up, suspected of being an accomplice. It is considered one of the most cold-blooded murders ever perpetrated in Old Catawba."

The Southern Home newspaper of Friday, November 18, 1878, outlined some of the evidence against the two and also pointed to a possible motive:

"The proof is circumstantial. McCorkle bought some shot a few days before the killing, and the shot was wrapped up in the Charlotte *Democrat*, and the wadding found in the yard is a portion of the *Democrat*. Intimate relations were supposed to exist between the negro and the woman."

The most detailed report of the death and arrests was printed in the *Charlotte Observer* on Wednesday, November 13, 1878, after McCorkle had been "adjudged guilty" by the coroner's jury.

"The evidence against the parties is circumstantial, and as to the negro is this: On the afternoon before the night when Wycoff was killed, McCorkle went to the store of E.L. Sherrill in the neighborhood and bought some shot. At the same time, he asked for some paper and was given an old copy of the Charlotte *Democrat.* Shot picked out of the body of Wycoff after he was dead corresponded with that which the negro had bought at the store. A quantity of the wadding shot out of the gun was picked up on the ground and the negro's gun was examined. It was found loaded and the load in it was drawn and the wadding taken out of the gun corresponded with that picked up on the ground – that is to say when straightened out and the torn pieces put together, an article could be read in the paper straight across the torn column."

Could a man who had been described as having "above ordinary intelligence" have been so dumb as to have left that kind of evidence behind – incriminating evidence that pointed directly to him as the killer?

Main Avenue in Taylorsville, a few years after the trial

And the man that committeth adultery with another man's wife, even he that committeth adultery with his neighbour's wife, the adulterer and the adulteress shall surely be put to death."
- Leviticus 20:10

Chapter Four

She Don't Look Like No Killer

Jesse Franklin Graves was an inoffensive, courteous fellow - unlike some of his pompous and arrogant legal peers – and had made his name as a well-respected country lawyer in the mountain counties of Ashe, Wilkes, Alleghany, Stokes, and his native Surry long before the biggest trial of his life.

He had entered public service as master of the Court of Equity in 1861 and had served dutifully in that job throughout the Civil War. When the court was absolved seven years later, he resumed his private legal practice, handling real estate, wills, and small-time criminal matters.

Serving in his first term as a Superior Court judge, Graves made a quick impression in legal circles across the state, and earned a reputation for fairness as a conservative, no-nonsense jurist who ruled with a courteous, but firm hand.

Graves directed his horse past a dentist's office, a tiny grocery store, the post office, and a two-story rock building where famed attorney and businessman Romulus Z. Linney had his office on the second floor. He pulled into a stall on Taylorsville' Main Avenue in mid-afternoon Monday, June 9, 1879, and after making arrangements for the horse's care at the livery stable, walked directly to Thomas Boyd's boarding house and tavern a block south of the courthouse to freshen up a bit before dinner.

It had been a hot journey on rugged paths from Iredell County where he had presided over an active court calendar. Now in Taylorsville, he was scheduled to hold court in the morning and preside over several minor civil and criminal cases before the cases of the State of North Carolina versus Robert McCorkle and the State of North Carolina versus Sarah Wycoff would be called in mid-week.

A conscientious fellow, God-fearing and honest beyond reproach, Judge Graves was not considered to be a brilliant legal mind, but no one ever questioned his integrity, and that was what was most important to him – and to anyone who faced him a courtroom. He came from good blood; his grandfather had been one of the most respected men in the Tar Heel State, Gen. Jesse Franklin, a former North Carolina governor, twice elected to the U.S. Senate.

Although politics ran deep in his blood, he didn't care for the rough and tumble life of a politician although he had served one term in the N.C. House of Representatives.

"He is an old-fashioned Tar Heel, and that means a heap. He was raised in these mountains, and he knows the ways and habits of the people. He likes them and they like him," a newspaper reporter recalled some years later.

After refreshing himself in his sparse room, Judge Graves read briefly from the Scriptures as he did every day. This afternoon, he turned to a chapter in the Book of John and these words stood out: "Judge not according to appearance but judge righteous judgment."

As a jurist and a man of wealth and privilege he sometimes had to remind himself not to judge defendants who appeared before him based on how they looked, how they dressed, how they talked, or even the color of their skin.

He closed his Bible, prayed a short, silent prayer, then joined some members of the local Bar and the Catawba County clerk of court for supper. The clerk had been summoned as a witness in the case, not as to the particulars of the killing, but presumably to confirm the details of pre-trial legal matters in the case. As was his custom, Judge Graves refrained from talking about cases on the upcoming court calendar, and his wish was respected by others at his table.

A delicious supper was served: fried chicken, lima beans, cornbread, fried okra, fresh cucumbers, and juicy tomatoes.

They exchanged small talk, complained about the oppressive heat, and talked excitedly about upcoming hog-killing time. Most of the discussion stayed away from politics, except for one brief exchange between two dinner companions about an Ohio Republican named Rutherford B. Hayes, whom one accused of "stealing" the 1876 presidential election three years earlier.

"He stole it. Plain and simple. The Democrats cheated, and everyone here knows it. The economy has gone to hell, and all they want to do is shut down the government."

"I strongly disagree, sir," another man replied. "And Hayes got the federal troops out of North Carolina, so don't blame him for every damned thing. Please, pass the okra."

Judge Graves listened patiently to the discourse for a few minutes, then quietly and with a smile and a slight wave of his hand, spoke up.

"Gentlemen, please. Let's just enjoy our dinner and each other's pleasant company and leave the politicking for somewhere else at some other time."

A few mutters followed, but everyone yielded to the judge's request, and the small talk resumed.

"Judge, tell us about those Siamese Twins, Chang and Eng. I understand you knew them quite well," one man remarked.

Judge Graves welcomed the opportunity to talk about something other than politics, and he was currently writing a biography of the world's most famous twins, so he offered a few words.

"Well, I will tell you this, gentlemen. Yes, they were cojoined, that's what they call it, and that's what most folks want to talk about. That's certainly understandable. But what most people don't know is this: they were two of the finest men I have ever known. Kind, exceptionally well read, devoted family men – both of them - and just good neighbors of mine for many years. Everyone thought the world of them. Good people, they were. Very good people."

The men listened attentively as the judge told a few short stories about the twins, their lives as "freaks" in worldwide circus shows, and how they lived like everyone else in Mount Airy "although, they were very well off, much more so than everyone else around them."

He loved to tell stories, and his friends often called him "Uncle Remus."

"I heard they used to live over near Trap Hill, had a farm there or some such before moving to Mount Airy," one fellow stated.

"Yes, in fact, they did. They were on a tour once – I think Wilkesboro was on the schedule - and they ended up falling in love with our mountains. Who wouldn't? Chang told me once that after all of the places in the world that they had seen in their lives – and they had seen many - the peace and quiet around Trap Hill was the most welcome to their eyes and senses, so they bought some land, opened up a general store for a while and raised corn and hogs. But that was long before I knew them. They later moved to Surry County and that's when we became neighbors."

"Tell us more, Judge. Most of us have never heard any of this."

"Very well, but just a few minutes more. Let's see now. Chang and Eng owned a number of slaves, and they worked them hard, especially the males until they got into their twenties, and then they'd sell them and buy younger field hands. But I digress. What a lot of folks also don't know is that Chang and Eng were pioneers in new farming techniques and grew a lot of fine tobacco. Gentlemen, it's getting late, and I need to study a bit and get some rest before court opens tomorrow. I bid you goodnight and I hope you understand," he said pleasantly as he nodded and arose from his chair.

"And a good night to you as well, judge. See you in the morning," said Solicitor J.S. Adams of Asheville.

Solicitor Adams and Judge Graves had spent the past several weeks in Yancey, Watauga and Iredell counties, traveling from county to county to handle cases in Superior Court. Adams had his eye on some land in Iredell County that he had looked over one afternoon after a court session in Statesville and told Judge Graves that he intended to purchase it and move there after this trial ended.

Tuesday, June 10, 1879

A crowd numbering in the hundreds shuffled impatiently outside the wooden two-story "modern" Taylor County Courthouse not long after the sun rose on a very humid early summer morning and waited for the doors to open so they could rush inside and grab a seat before the courtroom filled to capacity.

The trial of "that nigger" and "that woman" was the talk of Alexander County.

There was no talk about the weather this morning. No talk about hog prices.

"I damn sure hope I get inside," a middle-aged farmer in dirty overalls said to no one in particular. "I've been waiting for this ever since they brought that big-talking nigga and that Jezebel white woman from jail down there in Newton."

"Me, too," another man chimed in. "I hope they put a noose around his neck before sundown tomorrow."

"They ain't even got a jury yet," someone with a voice of authority replied. "Hell, for all we know they'll set his ass free anyway. There ain't no tellin' what a jury will do."

"That woman. Did y'all see that woman when they brought her to the jail a while back? Damn. She sure looks nice, don't she? Fine. Mighty fine."

"How'd she ever get involved with that ugly nigger in the first place?"

"You mean having some of that horizontal refreshment?" a toothy man laughed.

"I read in the paper that she'd been hangin' with him for a long time, sneaking around in the woods and such. They say her old man even caught 'em in the act once, but he took her back in like some kind of damned fool."

"I might take her back in," another laughed. "She's got pretty eyes. She might be a shameless hussy but she don't look like no killer to me."

"My old lady wanted to come here this morning but I told her there ain't no way. Ain't no way, I told her, that I was gonna let a God-fearing woman go inside and hear all them things no self-respecting lady ought to hear."

"Damned sure glad I didn't called for jury duty, but about everybody else I know around here did. The newspaper said there's gonna be 100 men in there waitin' to see if they get on the jury. Hell, they even called Isaac Lewis from over in Ellendale. Y'all know him? He farms some land over near the Little River Post Office. He ain't the kind of feller who'd even kill a rabid dog if he bit him in the ass, much less send someone to prison or the gallows."

"I wouldn't have minded bein' on the jury. At least I'd get inside and get to hear all of the evidence. Hope this gets over soon so we can watch the black bastard dangle."

The big wooden doors on the courthouse opened and the men pushed and shoved to get inside. Within a few minutes, the courtroom grew quiet as the spectators heard a strange shuffling from inside a closed door behind the bench.

"They must have brought 'em in from the jail. Probably in shackles."

"Y'all shut up Here they come!'

Four deputies – two for Bob McCorkle and two for Sarah Wycoff – quickly escorted the defendants to their seats where their attorneys already were seated. Bob nervously eyed the courtroom as his shackles were unlocked and he was directed to sit down.

Sarah was stoic, stared straight ahead, but managed to straighten her dress and push some hair out of her face as she took her seat and hung her head down. She looked miserable after months in jail, but she wanted to look her best on this day.

The courtroom came alive with whispers from wide-eyed spectators whose comments were loud enough to be heard.

"Splendid!" said one.

"I swear, she's too beautiful to have done such a thing," another chimed in.

"Look at that ugly beast," remarked another. "He looks like the devil himself."

The bailiff's booming voice immediately brought the noisy and packed courtroom to order as Judge Graves entered from the left door behind the bench.

"All rise!" the bailiff ordered, and everyone arose from their seats, all eyes glued to the judge as he sat down and began to shuffle some papers on his elevated bench. He didn't look at the defendants or anyone else in the courtroom.

"You may call the next case, Mr. Bailiff," Judge Graves ordered.

"Yes, sir. Oyez. Oyez. Oyez. The Superior Court of Alexander County is now in session. The Honorable Jesse Franklin Graves, presiding. The next case, your honor, is the State of North Carolina versus Robert McCorkle and Sarah Wycoff, both indicted on charges of murder in the first degree. This case was removed from Catawba County by order of   the court."

There was no sympathy in the courtroom for Bob. In fact, the *Goldsboro Messenger* newspaper later reported that when Bob's indictment was read, "hate, aversion and disgust was on every face, for Bob McCorkle was not only ugly, but deformed, and the bare idea of a beautiful woman consorting with such a man was abhorrent."

The newspaper reported that despite her months of confinement, Sarah was still beautiful and stood up straight "with an eye that flashed and a bosom that heaved. Those who saw her could but compare her with the negro and think of Beauty and the Beast."

After the indictments were read, the bailiff ordered everyone to be seated and the spectators quickly complied, shuffling into their seats for what was expected to be one of the most sensational trials in North Carolina history.

Judge Graves nodded and looked down at the attorneys and the defendants. This was not the first time he had seen Bob McCorkle and Sarah Wycoff. Three months earlier, he had been in Catawba County when the alleged killers had been arraigned for what the *Newton Enterprise* newspaper had referred to as "the killing of old man Wycoff."

On Friday, May 8, the defendants appeared before the judge in Newton, and he agreed with the defendants' attorneys to move the case from Catawba County for fear of not being able to empanel an impartial jury because of all of the sensational pre-trial publicity, much of it based on rumors and outright lies.

Solicitor Adams agreed with the change of venue motion and Judge Graves moved the case to Alexander County where they were scheduled to hold court in June.

Indeed, the Wycoff murder case had been not only big news in Catawba and nearby counties since the killing last fall, but it had also made headlines all over the South, with the *Raleigh (NC) News* being one of the newspapers paying special attention to it.

"It is considered one of the most cold-blooded murders ever perpetrated in Old Catawba," the paper stated.

Even the *Sedalia Weekly Bazoo* in far off Sedalia, Missouri, thought the story was newsworthy enough for its readers.

"The story of Bob McCorkle's crime is one of the most revolting and disgusting in the criminal calendar," it stated.

Judge Graves spoke with judicial authority and began what some newspapers were labeling as the biggest and most notorious trial in North Carolina history, a trial that would pit some of the most noted lawyers in the state against each other.

"Very well, Mr. Bailiff. All parties to this proceeding are present and we shall proceed. The state is being represented in this case by Solicitor J.S. Adams, and he is being assisted by Colonel R.Z.

Linney and the honorable Theo H. Cobb. The defendants are being represented by Colonel Locke McCorkle, the honorable George Nathaniel Folk, and the honorable Will G. Burkhead. All parties have previously agreed to the terms and conditions of this trial. Therefore, we shall now begin the process of selecting a jury."

Jury selection was slow, mundane, and methodical, and it consumed the entire day Tuesday. In the hot, late afternoon, Judge Graves adjourned the court and ordered all interested parties to return Wednesday morning to continue the process. By noon Wednesday, a jury of twelve white men had been selected and testimony got under way.

For the recently elected Solicitor Adams of Asheville this was to be his biggest case yet and he was wise enough to have enlisted the assistance of the very capable and experienced attorneys Linney and Cobb. Although they presented most of the state's case against Bob and Sarah, Solicitor Adams made the opening arguments and outlined what he believed to be a rock-solid case of murder.

He referred to the deceased as a kind, affectionate husband, devoted to his wife, long after she had shown him that she did not love him, did not care for him, and, in fact, despised him. He said that although they seemed to be a happy couple for several years after their marriage, Sarah grew increasingly less affectionate, and it was plain to everyone in the community that she was not only tired of her husband, but evidence he planned to present would prove that she was of shady character, and nothing short of a prostitute who laid with men of all persuasions including her codefendant, the negro Robert McCorkle, whom she conspired with to murder her husband, a simple farmer and carpenter named John Wesley Wycoff.

"Revolting as it may seem, incredible, too, yet this woman, still beautiful in her prime, was untrue to her husband and convinced, as was her codefendant, that Mr. Wycoff must be put out of the way – finally and fatally – so that they could openly love one another and, after a suitable mourning period for the poor widow, the lustful black man and the shameless white woman, his paramour, could be married," he told the hushed courtroom.

"The defendants deliberately and with deep premeditation developed a plan that ultimately would lead to the cold-blooded murder of an innocent man on his own homestead on the seventh of November last," the solicitor concluded.

As expected, he made no mention of Wycoff's repeated verbal and physical assaults on Sarah and how he had turned her life into one of nothing much more than that of a farm laborer, and the unwitting, unfortunate subject of his own demons. He said nothing about of the powerless, submissive woman she had become.

Adams then turned the prosecution over to Linney, a former state senator who had begun practicing law in Taylorsville about ten years earlier and had more courtroom experience than him. Linney would call dozens of witnesses in the next day and a half, and every single one of them pointed – one way or another – to Bob as the killer and Sarah as his accomplice - in what he called a diabolical crime of unconscionable, unbridled, illegal and immoral passion.

Witness after witness put together what appeared to be a tightknit case of murder. Linney began with the basics, some biographical background of all of the parties in the case, and then worked in witnesses who testified about their knowledge of Bob, Sarah, and what several witnesses said was a well-known illicit affair, something everyone in the farm community talked about all the time.

Testimony showed that John Wesley Wycoff was born from good family roots in Catawba County in 1828 and worked as a day laborer on various farms for most of his young adult life. By 1860, he and his wife, Mary Polly Saunders, had a two-year-old son, Charles, and lived with his mother, Elizabeth, near the Buffalo Shoals and Ball's Creek.

Two years later, on March 19, 1862, the thirty-four-year-old enlisted in the 49th North Carolina Infantry and was assigned to the "Catawba Marksmen" on April 16. Less than three months later, July 1, 1862, he found himself in the middle of one of the bloodiest battles of the Civil War and was slightly wounded at Malvern Hill, Virginia.

He was one of the lucky ones.

He and other members of Company I were cut to pieces by a superior Yankee unit. Wycoff and his battlefield colleagues spent a dreary, rainy night lying in a bloody field among the moaning and crying wounded, and the dead-silent fallen.

Wycoff recovered and remained with his unit and quickly returned to battle on another muddy, blood-soaked field.

The following September, his unit returned to North Carolina and was assigned to Ransom's Brigade. He was given leave, returned home to Catawba County and impregnated Polly before returning to his unit that was bound for Virginia. There, they engaged in numerous skirmishes, and Wycoff saw many of his neighbors from Old Catawba die from mortar blasts or shots in the skull or chest while they battled the Yankees.

In early May 1864, Wycoff was injured for a second time, this casualty suffered at the Battle of Spotsylvania. His injuries were severe enough to land him in the Richmond Confederate Hospital and he was transferred on May 25 to the Confederate Hospital in Salisbury, NC, only a short horse ride from his home.

Private Wycoff never arrived in Salisbury.

A few weeks later, William, his second son, was born on the farm in Catawba.

On September 1, Private Wycoff was listed as a deserter, but that fact was never disclosed during the trial.

The hell of war took had taken its toll not only on Wycoff's physical health but his mental health as well.

Polly died shortly after childbirth, and on January 9, 1866, John married Sarah Eller, twelve years his junior, a perfect fit for a widower with two young children.

Completing his verbal biography of Wycoff, attorney Linney the told jurors that the deceased owned a small farm in the Mountain Creek Township in Catawba County, and often worked as a hired carpenter who was required to leave home for days, and sometimes weeks at a time, miles away from home to subsidize his meager farm earnings.

Linney said that years before his death, Bob McCorkle and his family moved to a farm near the Wycoffs, and occasionally did some work on the Wycoff farm, especially when Wycoff was gone. He presented witnesses who said that Bob and John became friends and occasional hunting companions. Frequently, John invited Bob to eat dinner with the family, and was treated almost as an equal, something unheard of at the time.

Perhaps it was this familiarity, this sanction of a black-white friendship that ultimately made Sarah feel no harm in treating Bob kindly.

One witness testified that Bob's wife had died about six months before Wycoff's death, and he lived alone with his eight children.

"Do you think that the defendant McCorkle somehow killed his wife to get her out of the way so he and defendant Wycoff could be together and ultimately be married?" Linney queried.

Defense counsel immediately objected, and Judge Graves admonished Linney not to pursue that line of questioning. It was too late; the seed had already been planted.

It was now time for the prosecutors to provide the motive for their case. They had already established that Bob had the means and the opportunity. Now, they had to establish the motive.

Several witnesses said that frequently, as soon as John Wycoff left his house for a several-day carpentry job, Bob would show up. Under cross-examination the defense attempted to prove that Wycoff frequently paid Bob to do some farm chores for him while he was away on carpentry jobs in nearby towns, and therefore was at the home as a paid worker. Witnesses stated that they could neither confirm nor deny that, but again the prosecution had planted another seed: Bob often waited for Wycoff to leave home, and he and Sarah were criminally intimate.

Reports of an illicit affair between Bob and Sarah spread throughout the small community where secrets were seldom kept, the jurors were told. Gossip was the fuel of choice for many do-gooders in Mountain Creek, and in the case of Bob and Sarah, their secret became public knowledge, according to witnesses.

Public knowledge perhaps, but husband John was clueless, prosecutors alleged.

Witnesses told attentive jurors that Bob frequently stayed the night at the Wycoff house when John was away, and one even claimed that he saw Bob and Sarah in a compromising position in the woods near the house when John was working in a field nearby.

As the afternoon wore on and jurors continued to hear more of the same, Linney called a white-haired farmer to the stand to bring the case back into focus and zero in on the motive. The farmer said that he had known John and Sarah Wycoff since their childhoods and liked them both but grew increasingly weary of hearing rumors about Sarah's infidelity.

One day, he decided to confront John with the neighborhood gossip and told him that there might be some truth to all of the talk.

John was indignant and didn't believe a word of what he was told. He told the farmer-friend that his wife was always faithful and ordered him to immediately leave the premises.

"If you weren't so old, I'd beat you to a pulp," John told him as he chased the old farmer from his yard.

Four months later the truth hit John Wesley Wycoff in the face.

Post-trial trial newspaper reports stated that testimony indicated that John returned home early and unexpectedly one evening, and as he entered his house, Bob McCorkle jumped out a window and ran across the field into some woods. Sarah was undressed and turned pale when John entered the room.

"He then began to realize the rumors he had heard were true, and he upbraided his wife for her conduct. She feigned indignance, and then denied the charge," one report stated. "She said that McCorkle had simply come to the window and left some vegetables that she had bought from him."

The *Goldsboro Record* report apparently was based on words that John had later told his old farmer friend whom he had driven from his home months earlier.

"That is too thin," John reportedly told Sarah. "The woman then saw that the evidence was overwhelmingly strong against her, and she confessed her crime. On her knees, she begged her husband's forgiveness. The ignorant husband forgave her when she promised to sin no more. And she did this with tears in her eyes."

The testimony showed that John remained distrustful of Sarah in the following weeks and the illicit relationship became even more notorious in the neighborhood. Some neighbors, so incensed that a white woman was sleeping with a black man, talked about taking matters into their own hands. Presumably, that would be the night-riding Ku Klux Klan of Catawba County.

One neighbor testified that he told John that he needed to move out of Catawba County for everyone's sake.

"Ain't no good gonna come of this, John," he told him.

Testimony was introduced that one day John went to Sarah and told her that he was convinced she was still seeing Bob and persisting in her "evil ways," despite her tearful promise to be true. He told her that if McCorkle ever came to his home again during his absence, and he found out, he would kill him on sight.

A mid-afternoon witness, a black neighbor of the Wycoffs, testified that he saw the defendants about 10 a.m. two days before the killing in "earnest conversation" by an old oak tree stump near the Wycoff farm. Another claimed he saw them talking closely the evening before the killing near E.L. Sherrill's place. A timeline provided by the state indicated that the "earnest conversation," whatever that might have been, could have lasted as long as two hours.

An even more damning witness testified that he met Bob about 6:30 the evening of the slaying, and the defendant had his musket on his shoulder heading in the direction of the Wycoff farm.

Several witnesses said that they had occasionally seen Bob sneak into the woods close to the Wycoff's house, dressed in leaves, bushes and vines to conceal himself. He did this, according to prosecutors, "with all the craftiness of a red man of the forest."

Witnesses testified that Bob had told them that he occasionally hid near the Wycoff house to see if Wycoff abused Sarah.

"Bob said that if her ever caught him beating her (Sarah), he would drag him out, and give him a blue pill (a bullet)," one claimed.

Bob's old Army musket proved to be one of the state's strongest pieces of evidence and was the focus of numerous witnesses who said he always carried it with him. The musket had a sound that everyone in the community could identify when it was shot, and several witnesses – both white and colored - testified that it was the report of Bob's musket that they heard in the vicinity of Wycoff's house the night he was slain.

McCorkle's defense attorneys tried in vain to break the chain of the state's evidence and cross-examined the witnesses at length but made no significant headway.

The prosecution, having presented some very damning testimony and a substantial amount of circumstantial evidence, rested its case. Bob's life hung, literally, in the balance, and the scales of justice did not historically lean in favor of a black man in a white man's court, guilty or not.

At the conclusion of the state's case, Bob's fate seemed sealed, although his defense had yet to be presented, meager as it was.

Court was adjourned for the day.

Thursday, June 12, 1879

The courtroom was packed again, and at 8 a.m., Judge Graves called upon the defense to present its case.

One of the leading and most eminent citizens of Catawba County, Locke McCorkle stood up and addressed the court. It was ironic that Robert McCorkle's life depended in large part on the words

his former master of the same last name would utter in the next few hours and how successfully he might attack the testimony of the previous witnesses.

Words - big words, fancy words, colorful, emotional words, more than evidence - is what both McCorkles counted on to save Bob McCorkle's life.

Attorney Locke McCorkle

The defense would present no witnesses on behalf of either client.

The fifty-year-old attorney McCorkle was a veteran of the courtroom and had practiced law in Newton since he had graduated from Davidson College in 1843. He knew the ins and outs of courtroom procedure as well as anyone, and as a former clerk of court in Catawba County, he had more knowledge than most about how to work a jury. A former state senator and a member of the state's Constitutional Convention of 1875, he was also politically savvy.

He was known as a thorough, conscientious, and well-prepared lawyer, but his oratorical skills were weak. He would leave the word-weaving, in closing arguments, to Lenoir attorney George Nathaniel Folk, considered a consummate master of oratory and one of the greatest lawyers in the state.

The Virginia-born gentleman-scholar Folk had been practicing law in the area for more than a quarter of a century and had been a colonel of the Sixth North Carolina Cavalry in the Civil War. Interestingly, his legal opponent in this trial, Col. Linney, once said of Folk: "His powers of intellect are of the highest order, and his grasp of mind compares favorably with that of the greatest living American jurist. His speeches are like lightning, lurid and beautiful, yet powerfully strong."

Although two of Bob's sons had been summoned to be witnesses, apparently to prove an alibi, neither was called to the stand. Neither was anyone else. Defense counsel relied instead on strong closing arguments.

It was a fatal mistake.

Chapter Five

Guilty as Sin

Thursday, June 12, 1879

By the time testimony ended about 6 p.m., the state had called twenty-five witnesses; the defense had called none.

Throughout the torturous examination of witnesses against her, Sarah sat shamefully with her head hung down, occasionally weeping as tantalizing disclosures were made about an eight-year illicit affair that had ended in cold-blooded murder.

In contrast, Bob listened carefully with a brazen face to every word uttered by Judge Graves, the witnesses, and attorneys for both sides. He seemed unafraid, even in the face of damning testimony that was almost certain to lead to his death.

Judge Graves ordered that the case commence again at 8:30 Friday morning for closing arguments, and Bob and Sarah were put back in shackles and led from the courtroom to be returned to their jail cells. For all of the pre-trial fanfare, it had been scarcely a day and a half of testimony. Tomorrow, Friday the 13th, with magnificent eloquence, both sides would attempt to persuade jurors that theirs was the most compelling argument.

Although the evidence was mostly circumstantial and no witness put Bob at the crime scene, newspapers reported that prosecutors built a case so strong that neither defendant had a prayer.

A reporter for the *Newton Enterprise* stated that he saw "no chance for Old Bob to escape conviction" and that the "woman" will be convicted as an accessory to murder.

Friday, June 13, 1879

Shortly after 8 a.m., pistol-packing deputies separately led Bob and Sarah from the Alexander County jail and took them to two tiny closet-like rooms near the already-packed courtroom. Promptly at 8:30 a.m., the courtroom was called to order and final arguments to the jury began.

The distinguished Colonel McCorkle, "Marse Locke," as Bob called him, made a three-hour emotional speech on his clients' behalf, saying repeatedly that circumstantial evidence was not enough to send any person to his or her death. Bob squinted his eyes occasionally to help him listen more carefully, and he was convinced that Marse Locke would save him from hanging.

"This poor negro and this innocent woman have been thrust into jail and forced into a trial for their very lives without time to prepare their defense," he pleaded.

Colonel Folk, who was known as one of the state's best lawyers and most educated citizens, gave the final arguments for the defense. Like McCorkle, he waxed eloquently as he looked each juror in the eye, and cited numerous cases that showed the dangers of a jury convicting someone of murder based primarily on circumstantial evidence.

"Would you send your son or daughter to the gallows without any facts, and solely based upon mere circumstances that the state has joined together in an attempt to convince you of his guilt?"

Prosecutor L.Z. Linney

Colonel Linney, speaking for the prosecution, took only two hours to summarize his case, but he linked together the testimony and the circumstantial evidence very effectively.

He began his remarks in an unusual way, praising his legal opponent.

"My learned brother, Colonel McCorkle, who has just preceded me, painted in an eloquent and impressive way the importance of this case, and spoke of his clients, one of whom he referred to as a 'poor negro,' but he did not utter one word about poor J. Wesley Wycoff, who on the night of the seventh of November last, while sitting in his castle, which his wife, the female defendant, should have made an earthly heaven but instead of this, she had made into a den of prostitution, all of which Mr. Wycoff had borne for eight long years, seemingly as none could bear, and was decoyed out and shot down in his own yard, his own yard, mind you, a place where men have died in the defense of their wives, but few have died by the hands of their wives. "

Jurors listened intently as Linney continue to masterfully weave his argument.

"He was hurled before that awful bar without one moment to prepare to meet his God and only had time to say 'Lord, have mercy upon my soul.'

The courtroom erupted into cheers.

Judge Graves pointed his finger and waved his hand, making certain that spectators knew the cheers would not to be tolerated.

Linney said that Bob's motive for murder was similar to that of the Biblical King David when he sent Uriah into a fierce battle knowing full well that Uriah would be killed, leaving Uriah's wife, Bathsheba, to be a widow and subject to the king's pleasure.

Quoting from the second book of Samuel, Linney told jurors: "That when the wife of Uriah heard that Uriah her husband was dead, she mourned for her husband. And when her mourning was over, David sent and brought her to his house, and she became his wife."

That, Linney said, was exactly what Robert McCorkle intended to do: Murder his lover's husband, then take her as his wife. He also invoked the story of the notorious sexual encounters and adulterous affairs of England's King Edward II and Queen Isabelle.

Jurors were spellbound.

Finally, he quoted Shakespeare's *Othello*, and aimed his remarks directly at Sarah, calling her a "strumpet, a loose woman, a whore," just as Othello had referred to his wife, Desdemona.

Final arguments having been completed, Judge Graves read at length his official, and carefully crafted, charge to the jury. He wanted to make sure that this case would not be overturned by an appellate court, and certainly not because he had not properly done his job.

At 9 p.m., the jury went behind closed doors to consider the evidence. Bob and Sarah once again were returned to their jail cells with a jailer sitting watch nearby all night.

"Sarah? You there?"

"I'm here, Bob."

"Was that you I heard cryin' just now?"

"Shhh. We gotta be quiet."

"What for? I'm gonna hang and we both know it."

"Stop it, Bob. Stop it!"

"Sarah? I hate bein' this close to you and not being able to hold you."

"Me, too, Bob, but maybe the jury will let us go."

"No way. Ain't no way. Did you see the way they looked at us? Me, 'specially. That one feller's eyes – that old fat man – his eyes is full of hate. He can't wait to send an old negro to his hangin'."

"I said to stop it, Bob. We don't know what them jurors might do."

"Sarah? If they say we ain't guilty, will you meet me at the old stump back in Catawba?"

"Yes, Bob. Yes, I will. The first day I am out of this nasty old jail. If they let us go, we can finally get married, and maybe even move out of Catawba forever."

"Sarah? If they say we is guilty, will you promise me one thing?"

"One thing? What?"

"Promise me that you won't ever say a word to anybody about what happened. Not a word about anything. Anything. Promise me."

"I promise, Bob. It'll always be our secret."

"Me, too, Sarah, and please don't you cry no more. Please."

"I'll try not to. Goodnight, Bob."

"Sarah, I love you a mighty lot, a mighty lot."

"Love you, too. Bob. And don't you worry none. I won't never forget our promise. G'nite."

Saturday, June 14, 1879

Jurors deliberated throughout the night, and shortly before 6 a.m., they sent notice to the bailiff that they had reached a verdict. One courtroom courier raced from the courthouse to the boarding house to inform Judge Graves, and another was dispatched to the jail so that the defendants could be awakened and brought to the courtroom.

Standing once again before the judge, Bob and Sarah watched carefully as the jurors were ushered back into the courtroom and seated themselves in the jury box.

"Has the jury reached a verdict in each of the cases presented to you?" Judge Graves asked.

A tall, medium-age, well-dressed man stood up and answered forcefully.

"We have, Your Honor."

"And are these the verdicts from each juror?"

"Yes, Your Honor."

"So say you all?"

Each juror nodded in the affirmative. There was no reason to poll the jurors; their verdicts were unanimous. The foreman handed two slips of paper to the bailiff who approached the bench and gave them to the judge.

Without hesitation, Judge Graves opened the first slip and read it aloud:

"We the jury in the case of the State of North Carolina versus Robert McCorkle find the defendant, Robert McCorkle, guilty of murder in the first degree."

He immediately unfolded the second strip and read it:

"We the jury in the case of the State of North Carolina versus Sarah Eller Wycoff find the defendant, Sarah Eller Wycoff, guilty of accessory before the fact to murder."

The courtroom remained under control, but as the whispers suddenly became louder, Judge Graves put it all to an end.

"Sheriff, the prisoners are remanded to your jail and are to be returned to this courtroom promptly at 10 a.m. for sentencing."

As she was led away, Sarah glanced around the courtroom to see if any members of her family were in attendance. They were not. Shamed by her crime and by the embarrassment she had caused the Eller family, they had avoided the trial entirely.

Bob also looked around the courtroom and nodded at one of his sons as he and Sarah were hauled back to jail.

At 10 a.m., convicted killers Robert Bradford McCorkle and Sarah Eller Wycoff were returned to the courtroom to be sentenced for their crime. All of the jurors had agreed that death was the most suitable punishment for McCorkle, but they had disagreed on Sarah's fate.

Isaac Lewis, the 24-year-old farmer from Ellendale and father of an 11-year-old boy with epilepsy, held out for a lesser sentence for Sarah. He was the man a court spectator had said earlier "wouldn't kill a rabid dog even if it bit him in the ass."

Lewis argued for mercy and asked that Sarah be sentenced to life in prison instead of being strung from the gallows.

Judge Graves had a very restless sleep the previous night, but he had a job to do this morning. The judge asked counsel for the defense if they had any reason why his sentences should not be immediately announced. Folk and McCorkle told him that they had no exceptions to the way Judge Graves had handled the case and that they thought both defendants had received a fair and impartial trial.

"The only thing we ask, your Honor, is that Mr. McCorkle be given time such time as you feel adequate to prepare for his death."

Immediately, the ever-proud Bob McCorkle spoke up.

tide this District next Fall.

Condemned to Death.

The trial of Bob McCorkle (negro) for the murder of J. Wesley Wycoff, white, and Mrs Sarah Wycoff, wife of the deceased, as accessory to the murder, culminated in the conviction of both last week at Alexander Superior Court. The brutal assassination of Wesley Wycoff was committed near Newton, Catawba county, on the night of Nov. 7th. Bob McCorkle, an ungainly African of more than ordinary intelligence, was illegitimately familiar with Mrs Wycoff, a white woman, and who entered into a conspiracy with him to murder her husband. On the night of the murder Bob left the house of a neighbor living one mile from Wycoff's home at about 7 o'clock, P. M.; and the deceased was called from his house and shot dead one hour thereafter. The shot extracted from the body of the deceased and those found in the gun and pistol of McCorkle when arrested the next morning proved to be the same; also a

"Your Honor, one hour is long enough for me. May it please Your Honor to put me through right off. Don't keep me here longer than you can help. I am ready to taste the death other men have fotch for me. I've got no word to say against any of you gentlemen," he said as he looked around the courtroom.

Bob mentioned one witness by name (his name is lost to history) and said that he had a great deal to do with "bringing me to what I am at," but he neither denied nor admitted to killing Wycoff. He spoke briefly about how his life was being taken away from him unjustly and complained about some of the evidence that was presented. He rambled for quite some time and hinted that he had been set up by a white man whom he didn't name. While he admitted that it was his gun that had killed Wycoff, he did not admit to the fatal shooting itself.

Judge Graves listened dispassionately, then looked first at Bob, then at Sarah:

"This is the first time during my official course that I have been called upon to pronounce the death sentence. I am pleased to learn that the counsel for the defendants find no error on the part of the court. The jury having found the facts in the case it remains for the court to pass the sentence of the law."

He looked out into the packed courtroom and spoke clearly.

"This should be a lesson to all. Crime once begun leads to crime and may at last end as the crime of prisoner Robert McCorkle, who has committed the crime of murder, and society demands that his life shall be taken at the hands of the law, and the prisoner may well prepare for the doom that certainly awaits him. His attorneys have done all for him that science and eloquence could possibly do.

"Robert McCorkle, the judgment of the court is that you be remanded to the jail of Alexander County and therein to remain until the fifteenth day of August to a place of execution which will be provided between the hours of 10 o'clock a.m. and 2 p.m., and there be hanged by the neck until you are dead. The Lord have mercy on your soul. The sheriff of Alexander County will execute this judgment.”

Bob's legs nearly gave out from under him, but he regained his composure long enough to listen to the sentence for his lover.

“Sarah Wycoff, the judgment of the court is that you be confined in the state prison during the term of your natural life.”

Sarah and Bob then bid their attorneys farewell, were placed in shackles, and were escorted by armed officers back to the Alexander County Jail, one convict in front of the other. The walk back to jail was the last time they would ever see each other, although they would only be a few feet apart in their separate cells for another day.

Convicted of a God-awful crime, Sarah never saw her sons' faces or heard their voices again. The Wycoff boys were farmed off to relatives, and even though she wouldn't face execution, the shamed Sarah now faced life behind bars and was “dead” to the Eller and Wycoff families until her last breath.

Early the next morning, after having been sentenced to spend the rest of her young life in prison, Sarah was taken from the Alexander County jail by an armed male deputy and a female matron and driven by horse-and-buggy twenty-five miles southwest to the train depot in Newton. There, they boarded a passenger car on the narrow-gauge Western North Carolina Railroad, ultimately bound for the state penitentiary in Raleigh. Two minutes after climbing aboard, smoke and ash billowed from the train's engine, and it chugged away.

Ironically, its first stop was a few miles east in Catawba Station, the town where the now-deceased John Wesley Wycoff had accused his wife, Sarah, of "sashaying around" in front of men who had been sitting outside the train depot.

The train made brief stops in Plotts, Statesville, Third Creek and arrived in Salisbury about 2:30 p.m. There, Sarah and her escorts boarded another train that stopped in Lexington, Greensboro, Hillsborough and finally, as the late afternoon sun began fading away, the state capital of Raleigh.

The depot in southwest Raleigh was close to the North Carolina State Penitentiary, and the travelers were met by two armed guards from the state pen who exchanged some paperwork with the Alexander deputies and then took custody of their newest inmate. She would be housed in a huge pine-log stockade in a miserable state of disrepair on a 22-acre plot. It had twenty prison cells, several outhouses, two hospital rooms (but no doctors) and two rooms for hard-to-handle prisoners. There were no separate accommodations for women, although there were at least two in custody when Sarah was booked in.

Sarah looked out into the gloomy night as she was escorted through the tall pointy-top stockades where armed guards stood watch. She walked into the open prison yard and out the corner of her eyes saw a magnificent stone fortress under construction.

"What's that? It sure looks pretty," Sarah said. "I ain't never seen anything like that. It looks like one of those fairy-tale castles I used to hear about."

"That ain't no castle and this ain't no fair-tale, lady. That's the new prison, but you ain't going there," the female escort told her. "It won't be finished for a couple more years. You're going here, lady," she said, pointing to a run-down, half-block, half-wood structure. This is gonna be your new home for a long, long time. Quit talking now. Move!"

Sarah had no idea what was in her future, but neglect, lack of privacy, isolation and sexual violence were among the hardships she would face in the coming years.

North Carolina State Prison Inmate Number 1304 was about to begin the longest and loneliest years of her life.

July 15, 1879
Raleigh, North Carolina

Three weeks after she was incarcerated, a newspaper reporter was granted a tour of the state penitentiary and reported this:

"The Women's Apartment was first visited. Being Monday, it was wash and cleaning day, and the inmates were busily engaged in that pursuit that is classed next to Godliness. There are twenty-six female convicts at present, the majority colored. One entering with Captain Marsh and Mr. Roberts, under whose charge these unfortunates are at present, the party were looked at with some surprise, for it is unusual for strangers to be admitted to their prison. The negresses are for the most part confined on convictions of larceny, but now and then an occasional case arises like that of the woman, who in a fit of anger, threw her infant at her husband and broke its neck.

"Conspicuous among the females is Sarah Wycoff, confined on a life sentence for the murder of her husband. About the last woman in the world one would have taken to have been implicated in such a crime and for such a cause. Coarse, forbidding in aspect, it seems strange that she could have made anyone so enamored of a creature as to lead to murder.

\-   Farther On, But How Much Farther, Southern gospel hymn

Bob M'Corkle Hanged.

The Negro who Conspired with a White Woman to
Murder her Husband.

TAYLORSVILLE, N C, August 15.—Bob McCorkle, colored, was hanged here to day for the murder of J. Wesley Wycoff last November. Five hundred persons were in attendance, but there was no disorder. McCorkle spent the night before in praying and singing, and slept three hours only. He mounted the scaffold with trembling steps and could hardly stand for fright. He made a ten minutes' speech confessing his crime and bidding his hearers take warning by his end. His neck was broken.

Chapter Six

The Valley of the Shadow of Death

Friday, August 13, 1879

Morning broke, and it wouldn't be long until Bob McCorkle's neck would break, too.

He hadn't slept a wink all night and he welcomed the sight of the preacher walking down the short hall to his cell shortly after dawn.

"Good morning, Bob," the preacher said as he took off his hat and was led into Bob's cell.

"Ain't nothin' good about it, Preacher."

The door slammed shut behind him and startled the preacher.

"He's not going anywhere, and neither am I," the preacher told the deputy.

"He damn sure isn't, and I don't care where you go, but I ain't taking no chances with him. Not today anyway."

Bob shook his head. No, he wasn't going anywhere today. Not anywhere except the gallows, and from there, he didn't have a clue, but he hoped it wasn't spending eternity burning in hell as many wanted.

"Thank you for coming back, Preacher. Thank you so much."

The preacher patted the condemned man on the back and felt a cold sweat on Bob's shirt.

"You okay?"

"Okay as I'm gonna be, Preacher. I been a prayin' and a singin' all night but it ain't gonna make no difference."

"Well, let's try praying some more, Bob."

The preacher prayed a brief prayer, then led both of them in a recitation of the 23rd Psalm.

Bob furrowed his eyebrows and squinted tightly when they finished.

"Preacher, what does them words mean? That 'leadeth me beside the still waters' stuff?"

"Well, it means that even in the most difficult times, times like you are facing this morning, Bob, the Lord is still with you."

Bob nodded in understanding.

"Preacher, I gotta tell you that being dead don't scare me half as much as the dying. Being dead is being dead, but dyin' at the end of a rope, well, that scares me something awful, Preacher. They say my neck will snap like kindling wood and I'll just twist and dangle before I die."

The preacher swallowed back the vomit that was growing in his throat.

"Don't think about that, Bob. Think about tomorrow. There's a new day tomorrow."

"For me? Even for me, Preacher? A new day? Tomorrow?"

"Even for you, Bob. The Lord has promised that because you believe in Him you will have everlasting life," he said, hoping that his words of comfort might help.

"Probably everlasting in Hell."

"Stop! You *do* believe, don't   you?"

"Yes, sir. I believe, but I can't help but wonder, can I? All those years ago when I was workin' like a dog on Marse Locke's place, I wondered sometimes where the Lord was. And now, well, sometimes I wonder where He is and I'm afeared that I ain't gonna get into heaven after what they say I've done."

"You believe, and you have asked Him to forgive you."

"You think He did, or He will? Forgive me, I mean."

"That's His promise, Bob. You will be surrounded by angels tonight."

"Are there people outside, Preacher?"

"Lots of people, Bob. Lots of people. And more coming into town every minute."

"They're here to see me hang. They're just here to see an old nigger hang from a rope. They ain't gonna forgive me. No, sir. Not a single one of them. They don't know the whole story. They don't know what really happened."

At first, the preacher did not reply. Then he asked a question that had been troubling him ever since he had met Bob a few weeks earlier.

"Why didn't you tell them the whole story? The jury, I mean. Why didn't you tell them the whole story, Bob? The truth?"

"They wouldn't have believed me. It would've been my word against all of those white crackers. One poor, old, ugly, broken-down black man. My word ain't worth a shit. Sorry, I didn't mean to say that in front of a preacher-man, but this is still a white man's state. Always will be. Them Ku Kluxers are everywhere."

The preacher nodded.

"Bob, one other question. Why do they call your Doctor Bob?"

"Well, Preacher, I don't rightly know exactly. They've been calling me that for a long time now. Guess it's 'cause I was always a helpin' people, you know healin' 'em and such."

"Healing them?"

"Yeah, like fixin' 'em up when they gots hurt back on Marse Locke's plantation, and even fixin' 'em up in the head sometimes when they wasn't thinkin' right. Preacher? You think Sarah knows that I'm gonna hang today? You think she even cares?"

"I don't know, Bob. I honestly don't know."

"It don't matter anyway, Preacher. By this time tomorrow I'll be as cold as a wagon tire."

In mid-morning, a visitor was escorted into the cellblock, a newspaper reporter who had been granted the opportunity to briefly interview Bob before the hanging. Bob denied any knowledge of the murder but freely admitted to having had illicit relations with Sarah.

"I loved her. I still love her, and she loved me. Hope she still does."

He had nothing to hide about that. The affair between the former enslaved Bob and the pretty white Sarah was now not only a matter of public record, but also talk for gossipers far and wide.

The preacher and Bob heard a shuffling in the hall and the sheriff and a contingent of his deputies appeared at the cell door.

"It's time, Bob," the sheriff said.

"Are there a lot of people out there, Sheriff?"

"Thousands. Maybe two, three thousand. I dunno. I have guards everywhere, though."

"Lord almighty. Just to see an old negro hang. Guess they ain't got nothin' better to do. You say you got guards? For what?"

"Just in case someone wants to take the law into their own hands and deny justice ordered by the court or if you try to escape."

"Justice? What kind of justice did I get? And escape? C'mon, now. How is an old negro in shackles gonna escape and get away from here?"

"Let's go, Bob," the sheriff ordered, and Bob was led away, the preacher trudging not far behind.

At 12:10 p.m., Bob and his hanging escorts walked out of the jail and into a sunny day and the threshold of death.

"Good day for a hangin', sheriff," someone remarked.

Bob's pride and stubbornness began to escape him and he had to be helped aboard a wagon and be assisted as he sat on his pine plank coffin. He was then driven about a quarter of a mile east to the gallows, near a tanner's branch where at least one-hundred guards had encircled the area and were armed with every imaginable weapon. Hawkers, selling liquor, souvenirs, and food, worked the crowd.

Bob's shackles were removed and by this time he was overwhelmed with fright.

"He was so frightened that he had to be helped on the scaffold, and, while the sheriff was reading the warrants of execution, his knees shook, and he seemed barely able to stand," the *Goldsboro Messenger* reported.

On the ten-foot-tall scaffold, the now-trembling Bob joined black spectators, in what amounted to a camp meeting environment, in singing a hymn. Two prayers were spoken. Bob asked the sheriff if he could have some final words, and his request was granted.

Bob threw his coat down onto the coffin-loaded wagon at the foot of the scaffold and sang two hymns before he launched into a ten-minute rambling speech.

He always loved to make speeches.

Bob did not mention the murder directly but urged those listening to forsake their evil ways and avoid evil company. He said that his life was ending because of his passion for women, especially bad women. In a last-minute attempt at public redemption, he said that he had already suffered the torments of hell and wondered aloud about where he was headed after he was strung off.

"Goodbye, brothers and sisters. Remember me in your prayers tonight, for I don't know where I will be."

That stirred the spectators up.

"You will be in hell!" one white man shouted.

"You'll be in heaven, brother," a black man cried out.

A friend among the spectators yelled out to the condemned and asked him the question that many had on their minds.

"Who did it, Bob? Who killed old man Wycoff?"

"It weren't me, but I gots an idea who did. I done been betrayed like Judas for thirty pieces of silver."

He offered no words to back up his claim, then sang another hymn, bent over, pulled his boots off and tossed them to one of his sons who was watching the impending death of his father.

"I'm ready, now sheriff," he proclaimed.

The sheriff wrapped the noose, made of high-quality South Carolina hemp and wrapped in thirteen coils, around Bob's sweaty neck. The sheriff pulled it tight, but not too tight, and then placed a black cap over Bob's head so he could see no more. He adjusted the noose again, placed it on Bob's right shoulder, and then with one powerful swing of an axe severed the rope and sprung the death trap.

The rope immediately gripped Bob's neck jerked his head slightly upward, and his body shot through the opening and plummeted four feet down. His toes danced at the tops of the grass blades below him.

For ten minutes his arms and legs went through a series of revolting contortions, his legs dangling and dancing in circles. Spectators watched in awe as a man died in front of their eyes.

Thirteen minutes after he fell through the trap, Dr. J.R. Campbell of Newton told the sheriff that the condemned man's neck was broken, and he pronounced Robert Bradford McCorkle dead.

He left seven sons and one daughter and became the first man to be hanged in the history of Alexander County, North Carolina.

The State Penitentiary in Raleigh, N.C. was under construction when Sarah was incarcerated.

Chapter Seven

Her Lips Are Sealed

Behind bars in state prison, Sarah retreated to her old, compliant, quiet ways.

She kept mostly to herself and avoided any of the bickering and fighting that was common among the other female inmates. She was given a job as a prison seamstress and her stills were valuable behind prison walls. Those years of making clothes for the boys back in Catawba County had given her the experience and the skills to avoid hard labor like some female inmates who worked in the fields or washed the clothing of other inmates and prison employes.

In December 1884, she moved into the just completed castle-like structure that she had seen being constructed on the night she had entered prison. The new state penitentiary was finally open, and Sarah moved into her new dorm in the woman's unit. It actually felt like a fairy-tale castle to her after having been imprisoned for five years in the decrepit old structure a few hundred feet away.

All day long, day after day, month after month she sewed and mended clothes. Night after night she thought about her Bob and wondered about what might have been.

Friday, May 7, 1887

Morganton, North Carolina

A young man walked into J.N. Payne's hugely successful general store on Depot Street and ambled around the busy emporium, picking up items here and there, and just as quickly putting them back on the shelves or racks, all jammed with what Payne advertised as "cheap goods at the lowest prices in town."

Payne's store was particularly busy that Friday afternoon. Men, women, boys, and girls had to skirt around each other as they shopped its packed aisles. There were shoes, hats, ribbons, boots, and pants here. Fish, pickles, canned goods, coffee, sugar, lard, flour, bacon, coffee and eighteen pounds of rice for a dollar over there. In one corner, tobacco (24 plugs for a dollar), tinware, crockery and glassware were on display.

And candy. Lots of candy for the kids. Payne knew that candy would bring the kids in, and their parents would be right on their heels.

Part-time Methodist preacher and full-time merchant Payne was a friendly fellow, but he was tight with his money and cautious about how he conducted business. In between waiting on customers, he tried to keep an eye on the suspicious-looking young man who seemed to look a lot of items but didn't show much real interest in buying anything.

Shortly after opening his store the following morning, Payne discovered that some silver coins were missing from his cash drawer, and he immediately thought of that young man from the previous day whom he lost sight of while showing a lady customer one of the nice hats he had just gotten in stock.

Payne asked around all day, inquiring if anyone knew who his suspect might be and where he night live, and after church on Sunday merchant Payne asked Burke County deputy S.S. Lane to help him locate the young man he had identified as the thief. They found him near a crossing on the Western North Carolina Railroad and confronted him by surprise. He was thumbing through a cloth poke.

"What do you have in that poke, son?" deputy Lane asked.

"Nothing," the young man replied.

"Nothing? Open it then! Open it right now and dump everything on the ground," the deputy ordered.

The young man complied, and silver coins poured out of the poke.

"You're under arrest, young man. We don't take kindly to larceny around these parts."

Friday, August 19, 1887

Sarah Wycoff's Eighth Year in Prison

Raleigh, North Carolina

The train from western North Carolina carrying Burke County Sheriff B.A. Berry and his prisoner arrived in Raleigh in late afternoon. Convicted the previous week in Burke County Superior Court of stealing money from Payne's store, the convict had been sentenced to serve two years in state prison. His previous minor skirmishes with the law were enough to convince the judge that the young man needed some hard time in state prison to be properly rehabilitated for the error of his ways.

Sheriff Berry and his prisoner were met by two officers from the state penitentiary who took custody of the convict, put him in handcuffs and leg irons and hauled him off to the pen.

Sarah Wycoff had no idea that the young man who entered the same prison gates that confined her that evening was her own son, eighteen-year-old Jake.

By 1898 Sarah had spent nineteen years in prison, and her fingers - those tiny fingers that labored all day long as she worked as a seamstress - were beginning to hurt. They seemed to hurt more every day, and sometimes cramped up on her, making them hard to manipulate as she went about the delicate task of making and mending clothes. There was no use in complaining to the prison doctor.

Sarah still kept mostly to herself but was considered by the other female inmates to be more than just the longest-serving female inmate in prison; she was somewhat of a legend and was treated with respect and to a lesser degree, treated respectfully by prison officials.

In 1907 Sarah had spent thirty years behind bars. By now, her sixty-five-year-old aching fingers had grown gnarly, swollen, and twisted. She was not required to work so much anymore; she simply couldn't.

Friday, October 13, 1913

Sarah Eller Wycoff was seventy-one years old and had been behind bars for more than half of her days on Earth. On this day, someone special entered her life.

Like it did every day, a train arrived at the Raleigh depot before sunset and another prisoner was escorted to a prison wagon for the brief drive to the state penitentiary.

Sixty-seven-year-old Nancy (Nance Dude) Kerley, convicted of the second-degree murder of her two and one-half-year-old granddaughter, Roberta Ann Putnam, in the mountains of Haywood County, had been sentenced to thirty years of hard labor in the state prison.

The first meeting of two aged, female convicted killers was tense.

"What did you do to get them to put you in this God-awful place?" Nancy asked after she had been assigned to her room in the Women's Unit.

"What did *you* do?" Sarah answered curtly.

"I got thirty years for killing my granddaughter."

"You did *what?* Killed your own *granddaughter?* The Lord have mercy!"

"It weren't quite like they said it was, but my lawyer told me I'd get the electric chair if I didn't take a plea, so that's what I did, and here I am. Thirty years! How about you? What did you do?"

"I can't talk about it," Sarah replied.

"Why?"

"Because I promised someone I wouldn't."

"You promised?"

"That's what I said," Sarah told Nancy, and the words immediately brought back into her mind the night she had made that promise to her Bob so many years ago.

"Who'd you promise?"

"Well, now, that ain't none of your business, seein' as how we just met."

"Well, I ain't askin' you to tell me everything, just what you got sent in here for. That ain't too much to ask if you figure we're stuck in here together for the rest of our lives," Nancy responded.

"They said that I was an accessory to murder or sumpin' like that. I don't even rightly know what that means. I've been here most of my life. Don't know much else. My family don't even care. Ain't talked to none of them since I was put in jail back in Catawba County a long time ago."

"Are you lyin' to me?"

"Ain't no lie. Until you just asked me, I don't even remember what I got convicted for, and now that we're talkin' about it, I don't even know if any of my family is still alive. My boys might be, but my folks are long gone by now."

> Among the 21 convicts pardoned by Governor Bickett the other day, convicts "in whom no human being was interested," was one, a woman, who had been in prison since 1879. She was sentenced for murder in Alexander county and is known in the prison as "Aunt Sarah Wyckoff." She has been pardoned, or offered pardon, several times, but has refused, and said again when Governor Bickett pardoned her, that she did not care for it. "I want to stay here the rest of my days," she said. "My children have all forgotten me. I have heard from nobody I once knew in years gone by. I want to die here and be forgotten."

Friday, December 19, 1919

Sarah was informed today that Governor Bickett had commuted her life sentence to thirty years, meaning the oldest and longest-serving inmate in the state prison sentence could walk free. She already had refused pardons from several other governors, and there was no reason to believe she would accept the commutation offer.

Indeed, one newspaper reported that was exactly what Sarah intended to do:

"I want to stay here the rest of my days," she said. "My children have all forgotten me. I have heard from nobody I once knew in years gone by. I want to die here and be forgotten," she told the newspaper.

"She declared that the penitentiary was the only home she had, and she would stay on. She is 75 years old and crippled with rheumatism. Kind hands have made her as comfortable as possible. Her crime was committed nearly two score years ago. The law took her in her prime and now in her old age, she has no interests outside the gray walls that have hedged her in for a lifetime.

"She has not walked a step in twenty-three years."

Sarah declined the commutation offer and remained in her prison-home.

Chapter Eight
Aunt Sarah - Free at Last

By 1921 Sarah's medical condition had become grim. Now confined to her cot, crawling on the floor, or being pushed in a wheelchair by Nancy Kerley, her fingers were doubled-up in pain and the rest of her body was falling apart.

In February, Sarah gave the only interview known to exist with a reporter for the *Greensboro Patriot* newspaper. Here are some excerpts from his report:

"Aunt Sarah gave your correspondent an interview Friday. She didn't mean to be giving interviews—she doesn't even know what one means. She was reading her Bible, which is printed in 12-point type, and varying this with the scrawled letter which has come from her solitary relative, her daughter-in-law. The dutiful widow merely wished Aunt Sarah to know that while she has suffered in silence and mystery, the actual slayer of the old man, Wesley Wycoff, has confessed to the crime. Who he was, the daughter-in-law does not know.

"I am left alone with no one to live with me," she says, telling Mrs. Wycoff for the first time of her son's death. "Jacob is dead and gone and the children married off. He had six children—three boys and three girls. They are well as common. That man is dead that killed Mr. Wycoff. He told on his deathbed that he killed him hisself—that you nor Bob McCorkle never done it. He did it hisself and you and Bob was inosunt. I am glad to no and I wanted you to know the people had found out how it was done."

"Mrs. Wycoff is as ignorant of the trial and what brought her to prison as if she had lived in another guise and by some mental psychosis or other process had been transplanted from a star, the moon, or the sea into North Carolina life. She does recall that she had a husband; that she was accused of murdering him, was tried, convicted, and sent to prison.

"We were first tried in Catawba county. That's where they said he was killed by my Bob and that I knowed about it," she said. "And then we was tried in Alexander. It happened the same there as in Catawba. I don't know who the judge was, and I don't know why they tried me. They said I knowed sumpin' about it. They never said I done it, but said I knowed about it.

"She could not recall whether lawyers and the court talked about her being an accessory before and after the fact. All that she could recall was that it 'happened the same,' meaning that she was convicted.

"Governor Russell would have pardoned me 20 years ago," she said, "but there was no place for me to go. Other governors have said they would pardon me, but I haven't got no folks to take me. I guess I will keep on staying here.

"I would like to see Aunt Sarah get her pardon," her attendant (Nancy Kerley) said, "but we have learned to love her so that we want her to stay here if she gets out. She has never broken a rule and all the prisoners like her so much.

"Aunt Sarah seems to have 'satisfied the law,' whatever that means, and Bob McCorkle did his part 40 years ago. It isn't strange that the law has such difficulty satisfying Aunt Sarah.

It didn't take long for the Greensboro reporter's story to reach back to Catawba County, and as expected, the reaction was not positive.

AUNT SARAH WYCOFF NOT AS INNOCENT AS REPORTED

The Greensboro Patriot

"Hickory, Feb. 10, 1921 - Persons who sided in the vicinity of the Weslie Wycoff murder in the lower edge of Catawba county many years ago, were amazed by the recent stories sent out from Raleigh as to "Aunt Sarah" Wycoff, alleged victim of circumstantial evidence, receiving information several months before her death that somebody else had confessed to the crime for which Bob McCorkle negro, was hanged in Alexander County. Those who do not care to read, further may set it down that 'Aunt Sarah.' however well she might have behaved during her long term in the state prison, was not innocent.

"T. A. Sherrill, well known Hickory man, living within two miles of the Wycoff home, knew Weslie Wycoff and his wife and Bob McCorkle personally and got all the news in court and out of it as to the character of woman she was. Discussing her case Mr. Sherrill said that if the officers, spurred on by public opinion as they are today, had made half the effort to clear the mystery in the Wycoff case, probably a white man would have been hanged and 'Aunt Sarah' still would have gone to prison," the newspaper reported.

"The negro on the scaffold muttered something about others as guilty as he, but he did not give his white friend away. He never denied shooting Weslie Wycoff. McCorkle was found guilty of murder and the Wycoff woman as an accessory before the fact. The chain of circumstances was conclusive.

"To begin with, the court had a very bad woman as one of the principals. Her immorality was generally known, and it was practiced at the home of her husband, a good natured but worthless fellow, whose force of character did not commend to anybody.

Some white man in the community, whose name has been mentioned privately a thousand times, was believed to be at the bottom of
the murder. He wanted Weslie Wycoff out of the way and his
unfaithful spouse was a party to the conspiracy, the evidence
showed, that ended in his murder at his barn, where he was lured.
McCorkle was impudent, but not regarded as mean.

"When his gun went off on that fatal night, a man sleeping in the
neighborhood was awakened and remarked to his wife, 'That's Bob
McCorkle's gun.' By comparing the paper wadding shot from the
gun with paper found in his shot pouch, the authorities were able
positively to connect McCorkle with the case. He refused to make
a confession on the scaffold, but he admitted that somebody else
was in on it."

By the middle of January 1921, Sarah's health began to rapidly
deteriorate, and state penitentiary physician Dr. Joseph H. Norman
was summoned to her room on the top floor of the women's
building. In a faint voice, she complained of chills and fever, a sore
throat, and cough. Her skin had become blue gray in recent days,
and the persistent cough she had experienced since Christmas was
getting worse.

 Forty-two years behind steel bars and twenty of those being
unable to walk, Sarah's heart was very weak, and her twisted and
shriveled body was simply giving out. She hadn't eaten in days and

the once-stunning beauty who had turned men's eyes back in old Catawba was wasting away on her cot. She couldn't bend her knees even slightly, and Nancy kept a bedpan by her side, tending to her every need.

Sarah's mind had been slowly going for years, and in her final days, a crazy delirium set in. She began seeing things, hearing things, and her life in Catawba County came back to haunt her in one minute and comfort her in the next.

She was a little girl playing on the Eller family farm. She was a wife dutifully making breakfast for her husband and her boys in the little house in Mountain Creek.

She was taking deep breaths of fresh air on a cool fall morning and walking freely through crackling golden and rusty leaves.

She was sneaking to meet her Bob for a secret rendezvous. She was hugging him, dreaming with him, and looking lovingly into his face.

"My Bob," she would whisper.

"My Bob," she would cry softly. "I kept our secret, Bob. I kept our promise."

She saw John Wesley Wycoff's bloody body sprawled on the ground outside their house. She was sitting nervously in an Alexander County courtroom and hearing that her Bob would be hanged by the neck until he was dead.

She was trembling with fear when the judge looked her in the eyes and sentenced her to spend the rest of her life in state prison.

She was heartbroken because her family had abandoned her when she needed them most.

Shortly before he retired for the evening of Friday, January 28, Dr. Norman checked in on Sarah and shook his head.

"She doesn't have long now," he grimly told Nancy, who had been her friend and had cared for her the past seven years. Tears rolled down Nancy's face.

"Aunt Sarah was such a sweet lady who didn't deserve this," she told Dr. Norman as she picked up a tattered Bible that was lying on Sarah's bed.

"She read this every day, you know. Every single day. Sometimes she couldn't hold it in her hands, but she wanted me to read it to her, and I did. I reckon that means she read it, don't it?"

All day Saturday and until late evening on Sunday, Sarah continued in her restlessness, trying desperately to turn to one side or the other to relieve her pain. Her eyes were closed most of the time as death closed in, but they opened widely on occasion, and she would speak.

The words were always the same.

"Bob. My Bob."

Nancy was by her side throughout the final hours and tenderly shifted Sarahs' frail body from time to time to give her some comfort.

Sarah smiled weakly in thanks.

At 8:30 p.m. Sunday, January 30, 1921, seventy-six-year-old Sarah Eller Wycoff gasped her last breath, and Dr. Norman pronounced her dead.

Four male prison attendants entered Sarah's room where Nancy sat in a corner with her head bowed. They lifted Sarah's body, placed it on a gurney and rolled it down a hallway filled with tearful female inmates.

"Goodbye, Aunt Sarah," one sorrowful prisoner said as the death gurney passed.

On Monday morning, prison warden Samuel Johnson Busbee sent a brief, tightly worded telegram informing Sarah's last known relative that she had died. The warden asked Sarah's daughter-in-law, who years earlier had told Sarah of the death-bed confession, what the family wished to do with her body and where it should be sent.

Word came back from the family that the state should bury Sarah in Raleigh. No one wanted her.

Monday afternoon as her tiny body was being prepared for burial at the H.J. Brown Coffin House on Salisbury Street, Nancy Kerley watched as prison attendants made a careful inventory of Sarah's belongings and all of the things she had collected in her little room:

Three small aprons, all finished. One small apron that she had been working on before her crippled hands could work no more. Letters and postcards from people she didn't know. A well-worn Bible.

Three little purses. One for pennies. One for nickels and dimes. Another for quarters. They were emptied and nearly filled a quart jar. She also had on deposit in the prison office a meager amount of money, saved for more than forty-two years on a prisoner's income of no more than fifteen cents a day. It wasn't much, but it was enough to pay the undertakers to bury her.

Sarah Eller Wycoff's grave in Raleigh

"Aunt Sarah" Eller Wycoff, state prisoner number 1304, was buried on a cold, dreary Tuesday morning, February 1, 1921, in Raleigh's Oakwood Cemetery.

That same day, state prisoner number 17465 passed through the gates of Central Prison and was locked into a cell. More than 16,000 prisoners had entered the prison since the day Sarah had been incarcerated and many thousands had walked freely out those same gates, having paid their   dues to society.

In all of her years behind bars there was never a mark of discredit to her name.

Sarah had kept her secret and was free at last.

Society had been repaid, and then some.

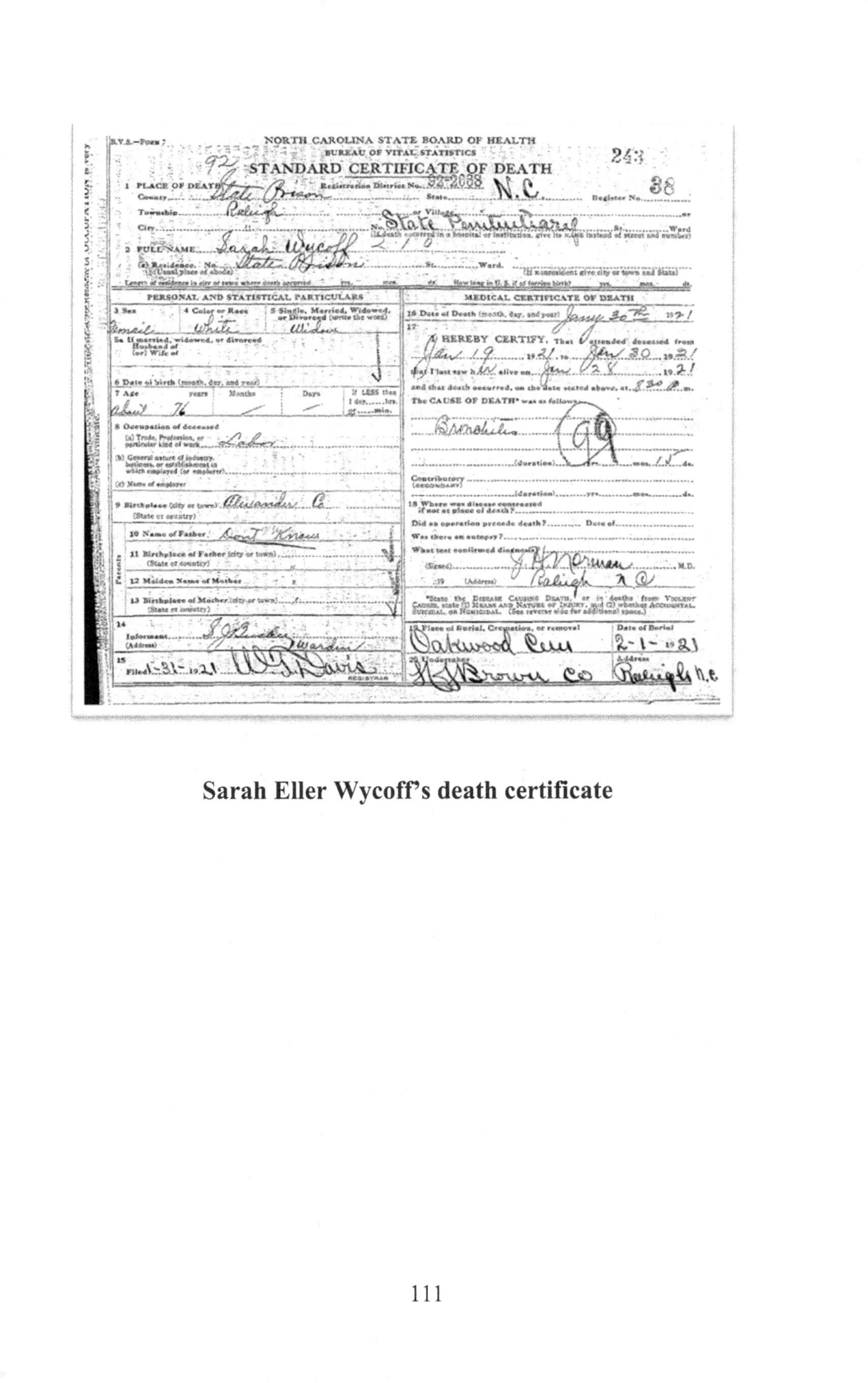

STANDARD CERTIFICATE OF DEATH

NORTH CAROLINA STATE BOARD OF HEALTH
BUREAU OF VITAL STATISTICS

Sarah Eller Wycoff's death certificate

AUTHOR'S ENDNOTES

White Beauty, Black Beast

- Eight months after Robert McCorkle was executed, Joe Gillespie, a black man from Iredell County, North Carolina, was convicted of murder by an all-white, all-male jury in the same Alexander County courtroom where McCorkle learned his fate. The scaffold where McCorkle died had not been removed and officials decided that it should be used again. Thousands of people from miles around arrived early on the morning of Friday, February 6, 1880, to watch the hanging. Nine minutes after his body was swung off, he was pronounced dead.

- On Monday, October 4, 1880, the sheriff of Catawba County sold the 100-acre farm that had belonged to John Wesley Wycoff. Sarah, who was his legal heir, had forfeited her right to the property, and a public sale had been ordered by Catawba County Superior Court. George Moss, a neighbor of the Wycoffs, paid $716 for the property.

- Robert McCorkle's son, Marcus, who was found not guilty of murder in July 1905, by a Catawba County jury, died two months later in Greensboro, NC of suspicious causes.

- Matthew "Marse" McCorkle, who defended the formerly enslaved Robert McCorkle, became a Superior Court judge and was instrumental in the formation of Catawba College. He died in 1899 and is buried in East View Cemetery in Newton, North Carolina.

- Nancy Kerley, Sarah Wycoff's fellow inmate and matron, was released from the state penitentiary on May 21, 1929 – eight years after Sarah died. She was eighty years old.

- Jacob A. (Jake) Wycoff, John and Sarah's troubled and only child together, was released from state prison after completing his two-year term. A few months later, an Iredell County judge sent him to the chain gang for another infraction of the law. Eventually, Jake became a cotton mill worker in Mooresville, North Carolina. He was forty-eight years old when he died of kidney failure and congenital heart disease on October 13, 1917.

- Charles (Charlie) L. Wycoff, John Wycoff's oldest son, never married and worked as a foreman in the weaving room of the Statesville Cotton Mill. He lived for many years with a spinster aunt, Martha Saunders, and was paralyzed for the last six months of his life. He died on June 19, 1923.

- The author has been unable to determine what became of William Wycoff after the conviction of his stepmother, Sarah.

HIDING
IN PLAIN SIGHT
The Two Lives
of
Kohler Holdsclaw

Chapter One
The Dead and the Dying

Thursday, February 24, 1938

Niles, Michigan

Frank Bentley didn't see the truck.

Cruising along the two-lane Michigan Highway 60 between Niles and Cassopolis, the giant tractor-trailer loaded with eighteen tons of paper came from out of nowhere. Icy raindrops in the night sky turned into huge snowflakes and fell with increased intensity, dimming his view.

In a heartbeat, the windshield of Bentley's coupe flooded with huge, bright headlights, and the truck cab roared through the split glass at fifty miles an hour.

Metal twisted against metal, glass shattered into slivers and the entire front seat was shoved into the back as the truck smashed and crashed its way through the car's cabin, then flipped on its side. A female occupant's head thumped against the car's right front passenger window, then crunched, and bounced back and forth like a Hawaiian hula-girl bobblehead figurine on a dashboard.

In the blink of an eye, the frosty night became still and quiet. The snowflakes grew larger and melted when they danced and drifted down into small puddles near the smoking wreckage. The hissing sound of a leaking radiator began to break the silence and Frank Bentley moaned softly, wiggling his fingers and his toes. They were still there. He wasn't so sure about the rest of him.

It was 1:30 a.m. and the beginning of the end for forty-two-year-old electrician Frank Bentley of Buchanan, Michigan.

Kohler Holtsclaw would not remember his 24th birthday. This was the day he was scheduled to die.

He sat in his dark and plain Death Row cell in the North Carolina State Penitentiary in Raleigh as a terrifying fear enveloped him from head to toe.

His date with the electric chair was drawing near.

He wondered how it would feel to take that long, lonely walk down the narrow hall to Old Sparky, how it would feel to be tightly strapped by leather belts into the thick wooden chair, and how it would feel to have that wet sponge with electric wires snugly attached to his shaved head.

He shuddered and tried to put the thoughts out of his mind, but the odor of burning flesh and scorched skin was always present.

"I guess I deserve it," he told himself. "I did kill that son-of-a-bitch, but he had it coming, dammit. He had it coming."

There was never really anything special about Kohler Holdsclaw.

Born on July 22, 1895, to Sully "Camie" Holdsclaw and Florence Sherrill Holdsclaw, he grew up just like all of the other boys living, playing, and working hard on their family farms in the tiny village of Terrell, near the mighty Catawba River at the extreme southeast end of Catawba County.

Actually, to call Terrell a village would be a stretch. It really wasn't much more than a general store and post office, a blacksmith shop, a church here and there - some of them rich in history like Rehobeth Methodist - and a little schoolhouse where children answered the clanging bell whenever their farm chores allowed them the opportunity to learn the 3 Rs.

One of the main attractions in the village of fewer than one-hundred residents was the cotton gin built by Miles Whitfield Sherrill in the late 1860s. The one-story, rectangular wooden structure sheathed in German siding, was six bays wide and one deep and was a beehive of activity during cotton-harvesting time.

Kohler had six younger siblings, four boys and two girls, the youngest of which, his brother, Freddie, was eleven years his junior.

As the oldest in the family, much was expected of Kohler, both on the farm and in helping to care for his younger siblings. Although complaining was not in his nature, he had a longing to wander far away from his daddy's farm someday. Far, far away to those places he had heard some of the old men talk about down at T.H. Connor's Store. Mysterious places like Texas, Oklahoma, and yes, even as far away as California where he had heard about the big gold strikes long before he had been born.

He had no illusion of becoming rich, but he yearned for adventure. Although the only skill he possessed was using his hands to work on a farm, he was exceptionally good at using them for just about any chore or responsibility he was given, no matter how simple or difficult. He worked once in a while at a nearby sawmill where one of his right fingers was mangled to the point of being stiff and almost useless, and he was fascinated with a newfangled thing called electricity that was making its way into rural western North Carolina.

Kohler was a quiet fellow, tall slender and handsome, and as he grew older, he heard from others that there was plenty of farm work to be had for anyone willing to put their minds and their backs to it once they crossed the Mississippi and entered those wide, open spaces.

That's what he intended to do until the "War to End All Wars" began and reached its monstrous tentacles across the Atlantic Ocean and into the red-clay farmlands of Catawba County, North Carolina.

On June 5, 1917, the twenty-two-year-old Kohler rode his horse to Connor's Store and registered for the draft. Store owner and draft registrar Thomas F. Connor dutifully wrote down all of the pertinent details on the form and Kohler signed it with a flourish. Unlike some of his farmer friends, Kohler was literate and never missed reading a copy of the *Progressive Farmer* that was delivered by mail to his father once a week.

Kohler had no desire to become involved in fighting a war in Europe, but then again, the thought of traveling overseas and the potential for adventure were tempting for a young man living a mundane life on a North Carolina farm.

Two months earlier, President Woodrow Wilson had declared war on Germany, and the call to arms had begun. Some young men enlisted; some were drafted. Nearly all answered the call one way or the other.

On Monday, July 22, 1918, Kohler Holdsclaw, along with nineteen other young farmers from the area, was ordered to report to the local draft board in Newton for induction into the United States Army.

It was his birthday.

By the end of the week dozens of other young fellows were on a train bound for Camp Hancock, Georgia, a huge tent cantonment that appeared almost overnight on 13,000 acres of sandy, hilly, fiery-hot ground near Augusta.

Private Holdsclaw and his soldier-comrades drilled, marched, and learned how to use the tools of war, from small arms to heavy weapons. By late summer, he was assigned to the Fifth Group for training as a machine gunner, and by then the epidemic of Spanish flu was consuming the camp. By early fall, more than six thousand soldiers at Camp Hancock had contracted the flu and more than five hundred had gone to their graves.

Kohler was of the lucky ones. The high fever, the dry cough, the chills, the runny nose. He had all the symptoms, and when a camp doctor diagnosed him with the killer disease, he was immediately hospitalized. While in his hospital bed, his unit steamed across the ocean to the bloody and poisonous-gas war zone to battle the troops of Kaiser Wilhelm II.

On November 11, Germany surrendered.

On December 20, 1918, the lucky Private Kohler was discharged and put on train for North Carolina. Back home in Terrell a few days later, Kohler went back to work on his daddy's farm and renewed an old friendship with Marjorie Bell Lockman.

By New Year's, they were more than friends.

> ## JOHN GABRIEL KILLED
> ## AT TERRELL, CATAWBA
>
> **Well-Known Citizen Of Mountain Creek Township Shot By Kohler Holsclaw, An Ex-Soldier.**
>
> (Special to Daily News.)
>
> Newton, Dec. 29.—John W. Gabriel, a well-known citizen of Mountain Creek township, this county, was shot and almost instantly killed today at Terrell by Kohler Holsclaw, an ex-soldier. The cause of the shooting could not be learned here.
>
> Sheriff Isenhower and a posse have gone to Terrell in search of Holsclaw, who is said to have fled.
>
> Mr. Gabriel was 50 years of age and leaves a wife and several children. He was for several years a deputy sheriff in Mountain Creek. The affair is a

Chapter Two
The Wandering Homebody

Throughout the winter and into the spring Kohler and Marjorie's relationship developed from friendship into love. They dreamed about building a life together, raising children, and, at least from Kohler's perspective, leaving Catawba County behind for someplace out west. Someplace fresh, someplace new, someplace with a future other than the backside of a lazy old mule or a smelly yellow jacket-infested outhouse.

Kohler was not much of a conversationalist, and neither was Marjorie. Often, they communicated simply by gazing into each other's eyes. Dreamers and young lovers have always done that.

Occasionally, Marjorie would turn away from him without any hint of what was bothering her, but he wrote that off as just a young girl becoming a woman. Sometimes, she would turn cold and silent and not pay him much attention.

There was always something a bit distant to her, as if she were keeping some secrets locked deep inside for no one to ever learn.

Again, he wrote those things off as simply the mystery of a woman, something his mama had told him about.

Kohler had his distractions, too, and was not always attentive to Marjorie. He often spoke of his dreams of going to California, and after having been as far west as Augusta, Georgia, he yearned to go further into unknown territory that begged him to go west, young man, as New York newspaper editor Horace Greeley had encouraged years earlier.

Kohler and Marjorie never became officially engaged but there was an understanding between them that when the time was right, they would announce their intentions.

As Kohler worked with his brothers and his father in a cotton patch near their home one afternoon, former deputy sheriff John Gabriel approached them. Gabriel, who raised chickens and grew produce that he sold at Connor's store, was not in a friendly manner.

"Kohler," he said, "I want to talk to you about a certain matter."

"What matter?" Kohler asked.

"Over there. I don't want to talk in front of your family," Gabriel replied.

Gabriel and Kohler walked a few hundred feet away, and Gabriel had his say.

"I want you to keep away from Marjorie Lockman," Gabriel demanded.

"Why?"

"No explanation necessary. You just stay away, you hear me?"

"That's not good enough. If she doesn't object, why shouldn't I see her?"

Things were beginning to click in Kohler's head, and he didn't like what those clicks were telling him.

The distance. The occasional mystery in Marjorie's eyes.

"Mr. Gabriel, I am a single man and Marjorie's a single woman. You are a married man with children. Why are you interfering with us?"

"I told you to keep away from her. You better take heed to what I am saying."

With that, Gabriel spun on his heels and strode away to his Model T Ford.

Kohler couldn't believe what he had just heard, and what he *hadn't* heard. The threat was clear enough: stay away from Marjorie or else. What wasn't clear was why.

There had been whispers in the community for years about what might have been going on, but never with earshot of Kohler. He always had somewhat of an innocence about him when it came to such things.

A week later, Gabriel was at it again. Kohler and one of his brothers were in a barn on the Holdsclaw farm when Gabriel drove up in his Model T and stomped out. Kohler heard the car door slam, and told his brother to stay close, but to let him talk to Gabriel one-on-one. They went behind the barn and Gabriel reiterated his demand, and his threat."

"Leave her alone or I'll kill you. Just as sure as we're standing here, I'll kill you."

He turned around and drove away, leaving a cloud of dust in his wake.

A few weeks later Kohler and Marjorie were returning to Terrell after visiting one of her friends when a car – a Model T - pulled into their path and blocked their way. The red-faced former deputy sheriff and well-respected Gabriel hopped out and got right in Kohler's face.

Gabriel screamed:

"You stay away from her, Kohler!" He pointed a finger in the direction of a shocked Marjorie who turned her embarrassed face away. "I've told you twice already, but you aren't listening to me, boy. If you keep seeing her, I'll kill you."

The "why" of Gabriel's threats was still unclear, but it was slowly coming into focus. Kohler got his answers the following day when he and Marjorie were alone.

A tearful, nearly hysterical Marjorie told him that when she was thirteen years old Gabriel had robbed her of her virginity and had been using her as his paramour ever since. She was "ruined," she said, and as the tears flowed, she begged Kohler for his forgiveness.

"You don't have to ask me for forgiveness, sweetie," he replied. "You didn't do anything wrong. He did, dammit. He did! That son-of-a-bitch will pay for this!" he promised.

"No, Kohler. No. You mustn't say a word to anyone or do anything crazy. He said he will kill you, and he will."

Kohler never once thought that she might have been a willing partner in the illicit love affair, and the tender side of him comforted Marjorie as she cried and confessed even more to her secret life with a respected married man with a house full of children.

He and Marjorie had never been sexually intimate, and now, well, now he didn't know what he was going to do, but he knew one thing for certain: despite the confession, he still loved Marjorie and wanted to marry her.

As the days wore on, Kohler's mind raced with a million thoughts and he convinced himself that what he really needed was some time alone, some time to think and sort things out. He told Marjorie once again of his dreams to go to California – just for a little while - and although she wasn't pleased, gave her tacit approval.

On his birthday - his birthday again - July 22, 1919, Kohler headed west with a promise to return as soon as he had seen his fill of the wild, wild west.

"I'll be back soon, Margie. I promise," he committed.

He worked along the way as a farmhand, with stops in Oklahoma and Texas where he bought a pistol for his protection. He was not a violent man, far from it in fact, but he didn't want to take any chances with strangers. A good traveler and a hard worker, he made friends easily. Ultimately, he reached California and picked butter beans and kidney beans in the San Joaquin valley until early fall, all the while posting regular letters back home to Marjorie. He was delighted when he received a letter in return.

By December he was back in Terrell and back in the arms of his sweetheart who was now staying with the Charlie Connor family, some of her now-deceased mother's kin. Marjorie was still unusually reserved and quiet, but they made plans to get married on his birthday the next year, July 22, 1920.

They told Onie Sherrill, one of Marjorie's aunts, about their intentions and urged her to keep quiet until they were ready to make the announcement. That was not the kind of news that could remain a secret for long in tiny Terrell and within a few days news of their plans reached someone who became enraged to the point that word got back to Kohler.

On Saturday, December 27, Kohler rode his horse to Connor's store and confronted Gabriel who was standing outside. He informed him that Marjorie had told him everything.

Everything.

"She told me of her relations with you and that I had better watch out."

Gabriel went berserk.

"You're right. I went with Marjorie," he confessed. "But that is nothing to you. It's none of your business. I had intended to take Marjorie with me and leave this county, but I have a family and couldn't leave."

"You have a *family?* You *couldn't* leave?" the incredulous Kohler asked.

"I've been like a father to her since she was thirteen years old and I have told you for the last time to stay away from her, damned you. If you don't, I will kill you."

Early Monday morning, December 29, Kohler went hunting with some friends and his cousin, Navy Holdsclaw, in a field near his uncle's house. Kohler realized that didn't have as many shells as he wanted so he asked a brother to go to Connor's store and get some more, and while there, to pick up his mail if he had any.

About 9 a.m., the hunters took a break and Kohler sat down to read a letter his brother had brought him. It was written the day before, and it was from his sweetheart.

Why a mailed letter, he asked himself? He would soon know.

The unexpected letter changed his life, Marjorie's life, and those of two families forever.

The words were cold and without emotion. Heartless.

Illustration by Don Komisarow

They didn't sound like Marjorie, but they were in her handwriting, and there was no question that she had written them.

"I cannot marry you, Kohler," she stated.

The words slapped him in the face and tore his guts out. He read it twice, then jumped up, tucked the letter inside his coat pocket and rushed away.

He went home, dressed in his old Army uniform, saddled his horse, and raced off to Terrell. Along the way he met J.H. Brotherton and inquired if John Gabriel was there. Informed that he was, Kohler dashed off in the direction of Connor's store.

It was time. Past time. He intended to confront Gabriel for the last time and hold him accountable for ruining Marjorie and destroying their planned life of happiness together.

What happened next depends on whose story you believed.

Some facts, however, were not in dispute: Outside Connor's store, Kohler fired one shot from his .32 caliber Colt revolver into the right side of Gabriel's head and Gabriel fell backwards, face down on the ground beside his Ford. Kohler then stood over him and fired another shot into the back of the man's head.

Kohler remounted his horse, waved his pistol towards Marjorie Lockman, who was at the Connor house about 125 yards away, and exclaimed: "Fare thee well, Marjorie!"

While a few stunned onlookers alternately gazed at Gabriel's body and at the killer Kohler as he rode away and disappeared, others went to summons law enforcement.

John Wilson Gabriel, the forty-seven-year-old husband of Carrie Howard Gabriel and father of six, never regained consciousness.

"He was dead when I seen him. Shot to death," coroner W.E. Wilson stated.

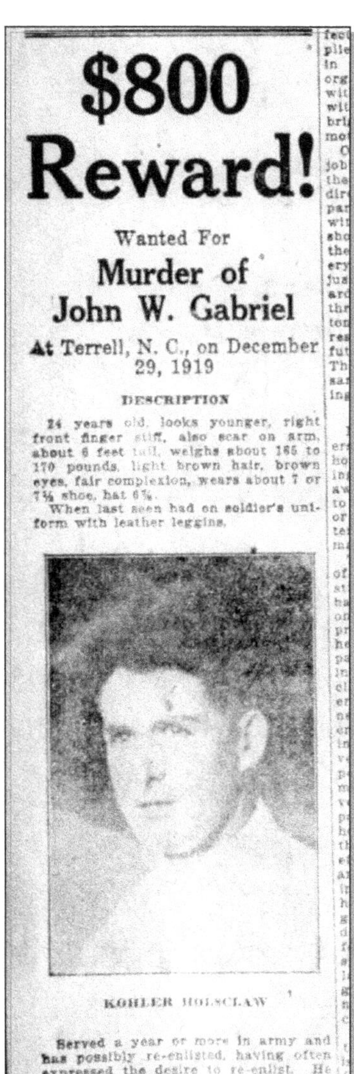

$800 Reward!

Wanted For
Murder of John W. Gabriel

At Terrell, N. C., on December 29, 1919

DESCRIPTION

24 years old, looks younger, right front finger stiff, also scar on arm, about 6 feet tall, weighs about 165 to 170 pounds, light brown hair, brown eyes, fair complexion, wears about 7 or 7½ shoe, hat 6⅝.

When last seen had on soldier's uniform with leather leggins.

KOHLER HOLSCLAW

Served a year or more in army and has possibly re-enlisted, having often expressed the desire to re-enlist. He has worked on farm and around saw mill practically all his life.

JOHN A. ISENHOWER, Sheriff
Catawba County
Newton, N. C.

The *Greensboro Daily News* reported the following day that the deceased was "widely known and esteemed as one of the best citizens of Catawba County. He was a son of the late John W. Gabriel of Mountain Creek and was related to many of the leading families in the lower part of the county and in Iredell."

Kohler pushed his horse as fast as it would gallop back to his father's house. He had one more thing to do before he left Catawba County for good. After tethering his horse, he ran inside the house, kissed his mother goodbye, and disappeared eastward towards the Catawba River.

Gabriel's body wasn't even cold when Sheriff John A. Isenhour arrived at the store and viewed the deceased. He quickly began to organize a posse, but by that time Kohler already had a two-hour lead on his pursuers and was making a clean getaway.

By mid-afternoon, bloodhounds from Mecklenburg and Iredell counties were on the trail, and the sheriff said that he believed Kohler fled a half-mile away to the Catawba River after the shooting, then got into the only boat on the west side of the river and rowed across the stream. Officers had to go twelve miles to cross the river and by then Kohler's trail was colder than a well-digger's ass.

Sheriff Isenhour said that Kohler somehow managed to hitch a ride once he crossed the river and had left the area. He then backtracked on that statement and speculated that Kohler might have re-crossed the river to throw the posse off his trail.

"I believe the young man might be headed to Texas where her formerly lived," the sheriff told a newspaper.

The search for the suspected killer resumed at the break of dawn Tuesday, and by then more than 100 men had been enlisted in the cause. They scoured a 10-square-mile area the entire day but found no trace of Kohler. Neighbors told the sheriff that they did not see Kohler at his father's house after the shooting and believed he might still be in the area.

The search went on.

The John Wilson Gabriel Family

The Gabriel family offered a $400 reward for his capture, and the state and county chipped in $200 each. Notices of the reward, complete with a picture of Kohler that Marjorie had given the sheriff, were posted in newspapers for several counties around, but days later there still no sign of the killer and no public comment on a possible motive.

Meanwhile, everyone in Terrell believed they knew what the motive was, but it took the newspapers a couple of days before speculating in print. The speculation ended on Wednesday when the *Hickory Daily Record* reported what the sheriff told a reporter.

"It was established beyond doubt, the sheriff said, that that jealousy was the cause of the homicide. Holdsclaw was in love with a young woman named Lockman, according to her statement to the officer, and repeatedly had asked her to marry him. She told him that she could not marry him as long as she loved another and asserted that she had been intimate with the murdered man for 12 years," the newspaper reported.

The statement that the middle-aged married father of six, including an infant girl named Adele, was unfaithful, caused an uproar among those who knew him, and they said that Marjorie's claim of infidelity must have been part of a sinister murder plot.

Kohler Holdsclaw vanished into thin air.

ARGUMENT IS ON
IN HOLTSCLAW
TRIAL

Newton, July 19.—The jury will not get the case of Kohler Holtsclaw, on trial here for the murder of John Gabriel, until Wednesday morning and a verdict is not expected much before noon that day. This became evident today when W. A. Self, of counsel for the state, spoke from 9:30 until court recessed at noon. He was folowed this afternoon by M. H. Yount of ccusel for the defense.

Other speeches before the jury are to be made by Solicitor Hayes, L. F. Klutz for the state and A. A. Whitener for the defense.

Another great crowd was in the court house today and interest continues great in the case.

Chapter Three
Murder or Self-Defense?

Six months later the long arm of the law caught up with Kohler who had been working as a farm hand near a relative's home in Auburn, Alabama since he had escaped the posse back in December. Catawba County deputy sheriff John Gilbert and another deputy transported him back to North Carolina without incident, and he faced Superior Court Judge Jesse Sigmon on

Monday, June 7, 1920, for a preliminary hearing. It would be his first time in a courtroom, but it would not be his last.

Solicitor L.F. Klutz, assisted by local Bar member W.C. Feimster, outlined the considerable case against Kohler. The evidence was overwhelming.

Noted defense attorney Amadus Augustus (Midas) Whitener, the Republican candidate for the U.S. Senate, represented the defendant, and he claimed that Kohler had acted purely in self-defense.

Judge Sigmon didn't buy the argument and he remanded Kohler to jail to await trial next month.

Wednesday, July 14, 1920

Kohler's defense team had little time to prepare for trial, but the day of reckoning arrived. It had been barely a month since Kohler had been arrested in Alabama, and Whitener wanted desperately to delay the trial or to have it moved to another county. He produced numerous affidavits to support his claim that he was not ready for trial. One of his most important witnesses, he argued, was in Tennessee, and another was ill in Terrell and unable to testify. Judge P.A. McElroy ordered that the witness in Terrell be deposed, but the court had no jurisdiction in Tennessee, so that witness was out of reach. He denied the motion to continue the case.

Kohler's attorney then produced an affidavit stating that the Gabriels were people of high social standing, very wealthy and influential. Therefore, he argued that it would be impossible for his client to get a fair trial in Catawba County. He moved for a change of venue.

Prosecutors were ready for that move and produced affidavits sworn to by seventeen citizens from all walks of life in the county who disagreed.

The defense's second motion was denied.

His next motion was his only legal victory, and it was a slim one.

When a pool of prospective jurors was brought into the courtroom, Whitener objected, saying the men hadn't been properly summoned by the sheriff. The judge agreed, the prospective jurors were dismissed, and Kohler bought another day before he went on trial for first-degree murder.

As soon as the judge announced that the prospective jurors were dismissed, he ordered deputies to guard the courthouse exits and tag everyone who came out. The case still needed a jury, and every man inside the courtroom was a prospect.

The sheriff managed to nab dozens of male spectators as they exited and ordered them to report to court the following morning at 9:30. Deputies then went out into the Newton community and grabbed every man they could get their hands on and ordered them to do the same. The next morning one-hundred men packed into the courtroom and jury selection got under way.

It didn't take long before the following men were empaneled: W.W. Burns, J.W. Shuford and W.T. Sledge of Hickory; I.E. Whitener, H.M. Wallace and M.R. Bost of Maiden; W.W. Trott, J.J. Cansler, W.E. Bollinger, John C. Scronce and A.D. Haren of Newton; and Charles T. Little of Claremont.

At 2:30 p.m. the State of North Carolina vs. Kohler Holdsclaw got under way. The *Hickory Daily Record* noted that the courtroom was filled to capacity with trial participants and curious spectators.

"No case tried here in recent years has attracted so much attention and been so largely attended as this, as both deceased and defendant's families are people of high social standing and scarcely can there be said that there is a bad citizen by the name of either Gabriel or Holdsclaw in the county."

The afternoon's witnesses for the prosecution were primarily those who saw the shooting or were there when it happened.

One of the state's first witnesses was Henry Gabriel, a cousin of the dead man. He testified that he was in Connor's store when Kohler arrived on horseback that morning. Gabriel walked out of the store and asked Bud Farrier, a young black man, to crank his car for him because had hurt his back hauling cotton, he told the court.

Gabriel said that the next thing he heard was the report of gunfire and went outside as Kohler rode off, waving his pistol.

"I heard him say, 'Fare the well, Marjorie.' "

Gabriel testified that he saw his cousin lying on the ground with blood flowing from his head. He saw another wound in the right temple with brain oozing out.

Quay Lineberger substantiated the testimony and said he was sitting on a bench at the end of the store when Gabriel came out and asked the black man to crank his car. Holdsclaw was waiting.

While the car was being cranked, Gabriel bent down to pull the flood wire with one hand and placed his other on the fender. The witness said he heard a shot but didn't know whether the sound was from a gun or from a car backfire. He saw Gabriel fall face first onto the ground, and then he said Kohler took his pistol in both hands, bent down, and shot the man another time in the head.

Wilby Gabriel of Terrell offered some more damaging testimony, and as one of the few eyewitnesses, was able to close some open circles in previous circumstantial evidence.

Kohler said calmly through all of the prosecution testimony and showed no reaction even after the evidence pointed squarely to him as a cold-blooded murderer. His parents listened to every word from their seats in the back of the courtroom as did Gabriel's grieving widow whose loud wails punctuated parts of the testimony.

By late afternoon the heat in the courtroom had become so intense that the judge ordered deputies to open the courtroom windows and place electric fans around the courtroom.

The testimony continued until early evening, and it was much the same: Gunfire. A dead man. A suspect fleeing the scene while waving a gun in the air.

The prosecution's case was cut and dry. There was no question who killed John Gabriel. Kohler Holdsclaw was the man who fired the instantly fatal shots. After establishing the means, the opportunity and the details of the crime itself, the state only needed to prove the motive. That would come the next day.

Late Friday morning, July 16, 1920, the state concluded its case, and after a brief lunch recess, the defense introduced numerous letters written by Marjorie to Kohler, all of them described as "endearing" in nature. The defense also produced two witnesses – Blain Sigmon and Henry Gabriel (the same man who earlier testified against Kohler), and both of them testified that they had confronted the deceased on numerous occasions in unsuccessful attempts to dissuade him from continuing his illicit affair with Marjorie. Each time, he told them to mind their own business.

The defense's star witness then took the stand in his own defense. Kohler's testimony was intense, deeply personal, and marked by a short delay when one of the most sudden and furious storms in years roared in from Hickory and tore east into Newton with torrential rainfall, high winds and brilliant lightning that caused power shortages in the area.

After the storm passed, Kohler resumed his testimony and finally told the "why" of the slaying. He told stories about how Gabriel had repeatedly threatened to kill him if he continued to see Marjorie and testified about the heated confrontation at Connor's store the Saturday before the Monday morning slaying.

"I told Mr. Gabriel that I had been going with Marjorie and that we were engaged to be married. Mr. Gabriel told me that I would never marry Marjorie, and he again threatened to kill me."

He then spoke calmly, telling the story of receiving the unexpected letter from Marjorie while he was hunting and said that he left his hunting partners behind to go home and retrieve a gun to defend himself if he ran into the angry and jealous Gabriel.

It was his intention, he testified, to go to Terrell to see Marjorie in person and to hear from her first-hand and without someone's undue influence, that she did not want to marry him. As he hitched his horse to a telephone pole near the store and began to walk inside, a motorcycle passed, and knowing his horse was afraid of the noise, he started back to the horse as Gabriel exited the store.

"As he walked out, Bud Farrier was sitting on the porch, and he asked Bud to crank his car. I was standing with my bridle reins over my arm. I looked around and saw Mr. Gabriel pulling a flood wire while Farrier was cranking the car. Mr. Gabriel turned loose the flood wire, saw me, and said 'Kohler, what did I tell you?' and reached under his coat. I threw the reins off and fired at Gabriel. Don't remember what I did after that. As I rode away, I saw Marjorie and waved to her, saying 'Farewell, Marjorie,' then rode home and left going to Alabama."

Self-defense, pure and simple, he thought, but would the jury buy it?

One witness – perhaps the most critical witness for the defense – did not testify. The witness Kohler needed most, Marjorie Lockman, was conveniently in Tennessee and out of the jurisdiction of the court.

Kohler stood by his story during intense cross-examination from the prosecution, and at 4 p.m. Judge McElroy adjourned the court so that he could go home to spend Sunday with his family in another county.

Court started a bit late Monday morning, allowing the judge time to return from his weekend with the family. Eloquent and long-winded closing arguments consumed much of the day, and one of the prosecutors alone, W.A. Self, spoke from 9:30 a.m. until noon. Lawyers from both sides waxed back and forth most of Tuesday and throughout Wednesday. Kohler's lead defense counsel made one of the finest pleas ever heard in a Catawba County courtroom.

Judge McElory charged the jury early in the evening of Thursday, July 22, and jurors were sent to deliberate the farmer-soldier-spurned lover's fate. It took them less than three hours to reach their verdict. They were nearly unanimous in their judgment as soon as the bailiff closed the door to the deliberation room.

At 7:45 p.m. Kohler Holdsclaw heard what he had expected all along: Guilty of first-degree murder.

His attorneys notified Judge McElroy that they intended to appeal the case, and Kohler was returned to his jail cell to await sentencing the following afternoon after Judge McElory had dispensed of a number of other cases he had to try.

At 5:45 p.m. Kohler was brought back into the courtroom.

"A jury having considered the evidence and having declared the defendant guilty of murder, it is the judgment of the court that the defendant Kohler Holdsclaw suffer death as the punishment for said crime as prescribed by law," stated Judge McElroy.

He then ordered Sheriff Isenhour to immediately take custody of Kohler and "proceed at once" to deliver him to the state penitentiary in Raleigh and into the custody of the prison warden.

"It is further ordered that said warden shall keep the said Kohler Holdsclaw in close confinement until the 24th day of September this year, and on said day, between the hours of 6 a.m. and 6 p.m., shall caused to be passed through the body of said Kohler Holdsclaw a current of electricity of sufficient intensity and for such duration of time as necessary, to cause the death of said Kohler Holdsclaw."

Kohler began to quietly weep, then louder as he was put into shackles. He glanced at his tearful parents as he was led away.

"May God have mercy upon your soul," the judge pronounced.

July 22, 1920. Kohler's birthday. Again.

HOLTSCLAW IS TAKEN
TO RALEIGH PRISON
————
Newton, July 30.—Sheriff J. A.
Isenhower and Deputy Sheriff Tom
Gilbert left yesterday for Raleigh
with Kohler Holtsclaw, convicted at
the last term of Catawba superior
court for killing John W. Gabriel at
Terrell on December 26, 1919, to be
placed in the state penitentiary.
Holtsclaw was sentenced to be elec-
trocuted on September 24th.

Chapter Four

On Death Row

Even though the Gabriel family was well connected and had many friends and relatives in Terrell, so did the Holdsclaws. While Kohler sat morosely his Death Row awaiting word on his appeal to the state Supreme Court, those friends and relatives joined with many other residents and organizations to come to the convict's aid, all believing that the death penalty was unfair for a man who was simply defending the honor of his betrothed.

Many elected officials, business owners and church leaders signed petitions that began circulating from Terrell in the east to Scronce's in the west. They requested that Governor Thomas

Walter Bickett, known as a compassionate reformer, commute Kohler's death sentence.

The Hickory post of the American Legion came out in favor of the commutation request:

"The American Legion believes in law and order. However, in this case about which this letter is written, we are fully satisfied that you should act promptly on behalf of Kohler Holdsclaw, for we are convinced that the circumstances of the killing were such that no governor on earth would permit the execution of the prisoner," the post stated in a letter to the governor.

The Rev. S.A. Ewart, pastor of the First Presbyterian Church of Newton, implored the governor and cited extenuating circumstances that, while not justifying the killing, deserved consideration. "It was a terrible crime," he wrote, "but I do not feel that Holdsclaw is a criminal in the bad sense of the word."

S.H. Farabee, editor of the Hickory Daily Record, made what might have been the most impassioned plea:

"You know the circumstances, Gabriel's infidelity to his wife and family, his sin against God and society are the main reasons why I ask you to show mercy to this wayward youth, who was crazed by jealousy.

"I have never signed a petition for a pardon and have never asked before that the sentence of the court be changed, but I have become convinced that this is an exceptional case and one deserving of clemency," he wrote.

Mrs. F.M. Williams, a widely respected community activist and former president of the state division of the Daughters of the Confederacy echoed all who begged for clemency, saying Kohler had killed a married man who had turned his sweetheart into a "common thing."

For five long, agonizing months Kohler sat in the shadow of the electric chair.

As the letters and petitions poured into the governor's office Kohler waited patiently for word from the Supreme Court about his appeal. Ten days before Christmas in 1920, the high court dashed his hopes and rejected all three points of his appeal. The justices stated that there were no legal grounds to reverse the lower court.

On Monday, January 11, 1921, Kohler was allowed to visit briefly with his parents, and it was in late morning that news came from the governor's office. In one of his final acts as governor, Bickett spared Kohler from the electric chair, but he would still have to spend the next thirty years in prison.

Overjoyed that their son wouldn't be electrocuted, the Holdsclaws rushed to the Governor's Office and tearfully gave him their thanks.

Kohler was taken off Death Row and was put to work on the state's developing roadway system. From February to fall he worked alongside other inmates to build the road from Durham to Chapel Hill connecting Duke University to the University of North Carolina. He enjoyed the fresh air and the relative freedom he had.

He was a good worker and early in 1922 he was transferred to the mountains around Asheville where he helped build roads across the Smokies and west to the Georgia state line.

A year later he was transferred east to a low-security facility in Mount Holly, less than fifty miles from his home in Terrell. Exceptionally good with his hands, very resourceful and a model prisoner, he was pressed into service to help construct a power dam across the Catawba River.

Mount Holly turned out to be heaven for Kohler.

He had visits from his family, old friends, and even from some old Army buddies. Often, they brought him home-cooked food and small gifts. A confined man has lots of time to think, and Kohler came to realize that a thirty-year sentence was better than death and he may as well make the best of it.

Make the best of it, he did. His prison record was exemplary, and the prison superintendent made him a trusty, meaning he had free rein within limits. The two years of heaven in Mount Holly ended abruptly when he was shipped to Caledonia, the largest prison farm in the state, where inmates worked thousands of acres of cotton, raised corn and other crops, and tended to cattle and pigs that were slaughtered to feed inmates across the state.

He was back behind bars in a stifling prison cell, but the wanderlust in him would not remain unchecked for long. The thought of spending decades in that environment finally became unbearable. Working in a cornfield until noon on Tuesday, May 27, 1927, he found an opportunity and simply walked away.

Free again. A fugitive again. But free.

Kohler walked for about a mile then regretted what he had done. His sudden impulse might have brought him freedom from a cell, but he was far from being free. Still, he could not turn back and spend months in solitary confinement - or worse – as his punishment for escape.

Mile after mile he thought about what might lie ahead, how he could never see or talk with his family again, how he could never speak of the past. In his self-imposed exile, Kohler thought about his life back in Terrell and about how much he had loved Marjorie. He thought about Gabriel's threats, the general store, the shooting, and life on the run.

And here he was again. Running.

"They think I'll head west again, maybe even to California," he told himself. Instead, he headed north from Caledonia, walking at night and hiding in fields and forests during daylight. He walked and walked until he reached the north and desperately tried to put his past behind him, but everywhere he went, every person he saw, could result in his confinement again. He was always on guard, always afraid that the truth would catch up to him.

Freedom was costly.

He assumed a new name, and by his birthday on July 22, had landed a job with a refrigeration company. He worked there until the Depression set in, and then he was laid off.

Chapter 5

The Whole Truth

Thursday, February 24, 1938
2:10 a.m.
Niles, Michigan

Frank Bentley and his passengers were extricated from the crumpled wreckage of his car on M-60 and transported by two ambulances whose screaming sirens pierced the night as they raced on the icy road to the Pawating Hospital emergency room.

An ambulance attendant feverishly worked on one of his passengers, but it really was of no use. Her heart was barely beating, she was unconscious, and it was obvious to the attendant that her skull was fractured. Her face was covered with blood that oozed from numerous cuts on her face and slowly dripped down her neck. She was limp when they pulled her from the car, and her hands flopped to her side when they loaded her onto a gurney.

It was going to take a miracle to save the life of thirty-seven-year-old recently widowed Gladys Schaner of Niles.

In the other ambulance, Frank Bentley, a dependable seven-year employee of the Indiana and Michigan Electric Co., and Rolland Rupple, also were being treated enroute to the hospital but their injuries were minor compared to Mrs. Schaner. Bentley's ribs ached, and Rupple had some cuts and scrapes, but otherwise they seemed to be okay. Bentley had been driving the passengers to Cassopolis when the accident occurred.

By noon the next day, Mrs. Shaner was still unconscious and in an extremely critical condition. Doctors said she had skull fractures, and the likelihood of her survival was slim. At the same time, Frank Bentley was being fingerprinted and booked into the Cass County Jail on a charge of driving while intoxicated. Still aching with rib pain from the accident, he was released on bond shortly after the arrest pending a hearing in Justice Court on March 11.

Mrs. Schaner passed away on Sunday, February 27. She never regained consciousness.

Friday morning, March 4, 1938

Frank Bentley's ribs were killing him, and he was having trouble breathing. Ethel, his devoted wife of six years, became increasingly worried about his condition and called an ambulance to take him back to the Pawating Hospital in Niles for x-rays and a checkup. Enroute to the hospital, Sheriff Arthur Shattuck pulled the ambulance over and quietly ordered the driver to take the patient to the McCutcheon Hospital in Cassopolis instead of the hospital in Niles. The sheriff followed the ambulance to the new destination, then waited outside the examining room for a while, before walking inside where Bentley lay in bed.

"Hello, Holdsclaw!" the sheriff announced, and Bentley's face turned pale, then relaxed.

"Yes, I am Kohler Holdsclaw," he admitted.

"You killed a man, didn't you?" the sheriff asked.

"Yes, I did, and let me tell you why."

Despite three broken ribs and what appeared to be developing pneumonia, Kohler answered every question the sheriff threw at him, and shared details of his twelve years on the run including the fact that he regretted walking away from the Caledonia prison farm just minutes after he escaped.

The sheriff asked him why he regretted his decision.

"Wasn't it better to be free?" he asked.

"Free? I have not been free. My every thought and action had to be guarded. Even my own name had to be forgotten. I couldn't communicate with those I loved. I had exiled myself forever, far from Piedmont, the land I loved. Never to be able to speak of the past again. Yes, to be afraid to even think of it. That was my freedom."

"Anything else you think I ought to know?" the sheriff asked.

Kohler did not hesitate.

"Yes, the most important of all. Early in 1932 I got married to the finest woman in the world. Yes, Ethel is truly a wonderful woman. But before we were married, I told her my secret. I told her I was a wanted man and that someday the law might take me away from her. She said she would always stick with me, fair weather or foul, and she has!

"For six years she was been the best wife a man ever had, never once referring to my past, always believing in me. I've got to go back and get this straightened out for her sake. I know she'll wait for me," he said.

Kohler said he would waive extradition to North Carolina.

"I killed the man in self-defense," he told the sheriff. "I'll go back. I want to go back. I want a chance to tell my story."

The sheriff took no chances and placed an armed guard outside the room to keep an eye on the former fugitive.

The headlines in the afternoon newspapers shouted the big story of the day:

Records Reveal Trusted Citizen is Escaped Killer

Alleged Murder Fugitive Seized in Niles Today

Resident of Buchanan is a Murderer

Buchanan Man Seized as Escaped Felon

Sheriff Shattuck told *The Battle Creek Inquirer* newspaper that a routine fingerprint check with the FBI after Bentley's arrest had revealed that he was Kohler, the fugitive who had escaped from the Caledonia, North Carolina, prison farm twelve years earlier.

"Shattuck said Bentley drifted to Buchanan where he got a job with the electric company, married a Michigan City, Ind., girl and settled down. The sheriff said Bentley had a reputation in Buchanan as a 'trusted, reliable and honest citizen.' "

Kohler was back behind bars the next day, but just like it had happened in Catawba County more than two decades earlier, a movement of supportive citizens was already under way to save a popular fellow whose reputation, they said, was above reproach. The petitioners, including many of his co-workers, said that Kohler was a model citizen who simply killed a man in self-defense, and was a model state prisoner – a trusty, in fact - when he walked away from prison twelve years earlier.

Hundreds of residents signed petitions to Michigan Governor Frank D. Fitzgerald urging him to stop the extradition of their adopted son to North Carolina, and other petitions were sent to

Governor Clyde Hoey in North Carolina, urging him to give Kohler a break. Many urged Kohler to fight extradition, and although appreciative of their efforts, he told his family, including his sister, Anna, who had just arrived from North Carolina, that was not interested in doing anything other than going back to Tar Heel State to straighten things out.

The petition-drives were led by the Rev. and Mrs. J.J. Terry with whom Kohler had lived as a tenant for three years before his marriage to Ethel.

"If Governor Hoey will listen to the story and learn what kind of man Holdsclaw has become, perhaps he will extend clemency," attorney Philip C. Landisman said.

While visiting with her husband on the second-floor solitary cell of the Cass County Jail, Ethel asked him what she wanted him to do.

"I'll go back and get this thing all cleared up and then we can start over again," he promised. "I'm going to see this thing through."

For twelve years no one other than Ethel had any idea that Frank Bentley was a wanted killer. It was their secret.

He was a quiet, unassuming, hard-working man who even hunted deer occasionally with two deputies. Nothing he ever said or did gave anyone the slightest suspicion that he was anyone other than the likeable Frank, a small-   town blue-collar worker.

On Thursday night, March 10, 1920, Ethel fervently kissed him goodbye and two officers from North Carolina, including Lieutenant A.T. Moore, took custody of him and placed their prisoner in a cell in Raleigh's Central Prison on Sunday evening.

Twelve years of freedom were behind him and the possibility of twenty more years in prison lie ahead.

His secret life in Michigan turned into headlines in North Carolina where petitions from Michigan began arriving on the governor's desk even before Kohler was back in the state. Michigan governor Frank Murphy soon added his name and influence to those asking North Carolina's top executive to set Kohler free so he could return home to Ethel and his life in Michigan.

Ethel wrote a letter to Florence Holdsclaw, Kohler's mother.

"I married him six years ago and I have never had reason to regret my marriage. Kohler has always been a prince to me, and I would feel very much ashamed if I did not remain loyal to him now," she wrote.

"Not only did he secure and keep my respect, but during his twelve years here, he earned the full respect of the people of this city. He has been considered a responsible and kind citizen, doing his work faithfully, paying his debts and performing other obligations faithfully."

"It has been suggested to me that you might cooperate with us from that end by petitions or otherwise to help us save him from lifelong imprisonment It might help us much. I have always known him as Frank Bentley, and so I am signing myself,

"MRS. FRANK BENTLEY."

While Kohler's friends and family were lobbying for clemency, the family of the man he killed, John W. Gabriel, were just as adamant against giving him any breaks and hired an attorney to take their case to the governor. They asked the governor for the chance to be heard if clemency was considered. Gov. Hoey told them had not had time to study the case but would refer it to state parole commissioner Edwin Gill for a thorough review after he had considered all of the history.

The Gabriel family attorney appeared before a hearing on Thursday, May 20, 1939, and argued vehemently against letting Kohler go free.

"We maintain that Holdsclaw was guilty of murder in the first degree and should not be paroled," he argued.

An editorial in the *Greensboro Record* cited the history of the case and reminded its readers that Kohler had killed a man, even if it was under very unusual and perhaps understandable circumstances.

"There is no denying that Kohler Holdsclaw killed. He sent two bullets ripping through the brain of his victim. . . . but is there no virtue in repentance, no reward for reformation? Is it not to be considered, in deciding this issue, that Holdsclaw has for all these years been proving his value as a useful citizen and that he has been a loving and provident husband to the wife in Michigan who has known him as Frank Bentley?" the editorial asked.

Which plea would persuade Governor Hoey? For months, Kohler languished in prison awaiting word. Three contentious hearings were held before the state parole commission, even one in which state prison officials praised Kohler for his "meritorious" service working day and night to help the evacuation of flood refugees near the prison farm in Caledonia shortly before he escaped.

Still, he received no word.

He wrote letters to Ethel, and she wrote back. He promised to return home to Michigan, and she promised to be waiting.

On Saturday morning, Aug. 31, 1940, he learned his fate. The *Statesville Record and Landmark* captured it perfectly:

"Kohler Holdsclaw, once sentenced to die in the electric chair for slaying his sweetheart's married suitor, was paroled today by Governor Huey.

"The 44-year-old prisoner was granted his freedom by the Governor because of the exemplary life he had led as a fugitive in Michigan after escaping in 1927.

Pays Debt To Society; Is Paroled

FRANK BENTLEY AND WIFE

BUCHANAN, Aug. 31 (Special)—
Frank Bentley, well known Buchanan resident for eight years and a service man for a utility company was paroled from the North Carolina state prison Friday, accord-

(Continued on page 9)

"Parole Commissioner Edwin Gill said Holdsclaw was being paroled to Michigan authorities in order that he may return to his wife in Buchanan and resume the life that won him friends and good reputation there."

On Sunday morning, September 1, 1940, the prison career, and fugitive life of Kohler Holdsclaw that had begun more than twenty years earlier, ended when he walked out the doors of Central Prison and headed home to Michigan. He spoke to reporters as he left and thanked the people of Michigan and those in North Carolina who had supported him. He was especially grateful to the governor who set him free.

The second life of Kohler Holdsclaw had ended. It was time for his third life to begin.

Frank and Ethel Bentley after his release from prison

AUTHOR'S END NOTES
Hiding in Plain Sight

- Kohler Holdsclaw, aka Frank Bentley, returned to his wife, Ethel, in Buchanan, Michigan, and to his job at the electric utility.

- He resumed his quiet life, kept mostly to himself, and never again used his given name Holdsclaw. He was often seen by neighbors working in his yard on Cayuga Street, even after his retirement.

- He never crossed paths with the law again and died at 6:02 a.m. Sunday, Oct. 29, 1972, in the same hospital where he had been arrested in 1938. He was 77 years old.

- Ethel predeceased him in 1967. They are buried side-by-side in Buchanan's Oak Ridge Cemetery.

- Marjorie Lockman has virtually disappeared from history. In a May 1926 Catawba County, North Carolina, probate court record she was listed along with a sister, Bertha Lockman Setzer, as heirs to their father's estimated $270 estate. After extensive research, the author could find no records of her or any people with knowledge of her.

Other books by Ken H. Fortenberry

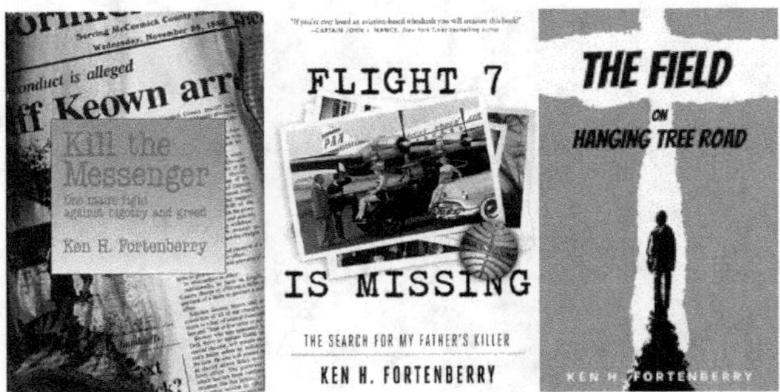

FLIGHT 7 IS MISSING: The Search for My Father's Killer

The author was six years old when his pilot-father left their San Francisco home and never returned. Eight years later he began a one-man lifelong journey of detective work to determine why his father's plane simply vanished without warning in the middle of the Pacific Ocean. "This is a torture of cold trails, frightened relatives, and the heroism of a loving son who refused to give up. **This is a must-read!"** - John J. Nance, *New York Times* bestselling author.

THE FIELD ON HANGING TREE ROAD

The scene is South Carolina during the turbulent and racially charged 1960s. Follow high school jock Brian Anderson on his journey from reckless teen-aged shenanigans, into the jungles of Vietnam and finally into the scandalous world of Palmetto State politics. More than a coming-of-age novella that takes you back to the stormy 60s, this book alternately tugs at your heartstrings and boils your blood. Romance. Hatred. Murder. War. Dirty politics. This book has it all.

KILL THE MESSENGER

The author's true account as a crusading newspaper editor in South Carolina is a powerful read. He left Florida to buy the McCormick Messenger, located in what he describes as one of the most backward counties in South Carolina, a land of good ol' boys who wanted no boat rockers in their community. When he investigated the local sheriff, trouble began. Advertisers pulled out of the paper, his family was ostracized, his children were harassed at school. His crusade succeeded in unseating two successive sheriffs, and when bombs were set off on his property, his family became worldwide news.

All of Ken's books are available on Amazon.com
or buy a book he will personally sign at www.kenfortenberry.com

ABOUT THE AUTHOR

Ken H. Fortenberry has earned hundreds of state, regional and national awards for journalism excellence including the National Sigma Delta Chi Bronze Medallion in Public Service and the  American Bar Association's Silver Gavel Award for a series he edited and directed that led to changes in teacher hiring laws in more than 30 states.

Both the Georgia and the South Carolina Press Associations have awarded him their prestigious Freedom of Information awards for his courageous investigative reporting.

He gained international national recognition in 1987 when his house was rocked by two explosions because of stories he published in the *McCormick* (S.C.) *Messenger.*

His coverage of corruption in local law enforcement led to a federal prison term for the sheriff, the bribery conviction of the sheriff's replacement, the exposure of the chief deputy as an ex-convict, and changes in state law enforcement certification.

He was featured on the CBS News program *60 Minutes*, the NBC *Today* show, and his story was reported by United Press International, the Associated Press and in dozens of publications including *Newsweek, The New York Times* and *Pravda..*

A former member of the Board of Visitors of the University of Alabama's College of Communications, he is a past chairman of the Southern Newspaper Publishers Association Editorial Committee and a former member of the Board of Publications at the University of Southern Mississippi. Ken is an alumni of Leadership Florida.

He was the first president and founder of the Denver (NC) Area Business Association and was named Denver's Citizen of the Year in 2003.

Ken grew up in Spartanburg, SC; Miami, Florida; the San Francisco Peninsula area; and in Bad Tolz, a small town in the Bavarian Alps of Germany.

A Vietnam-era U.S. Army veteran, he began his professional writing career in North Carolina where he met his future wife, the former Anna Jonas, and they were married in 1975. He has edited and published newspapers in both Carolinas, Alabama, Georgia, Tennessee, Mississippi and Florida.

His hobbies include trout fishing, camping, traveling, genealogy, and historical research.

Ken and Anna live in Macon, Georgia, and have five children, eleven grandchildren and one great-grand child.

For more information go to www.kenfortenberry.com